Helping Children with Yoga

A guide for parents and teachers

Michelle Cheesbrough and Sarah Woodhouse

with Rosemary Griffiths

A Right from the Start book

Published by Network Continuum Education
The Tower Building, 11 York Road
London SE1 7NX

www.networkcontinuum.co.uk
www.continuumbooks.com

An imprint of The Continuum International Publishing Group Ltd

First published 2006
© Michelle Cheesbrough, Sarah Woodhouse and Rosemary Griffiths 2006

ISBN-13:   978 185539 220 5
ISBN-10:   185539 220 8

The exercises in this book are safe provided the instructions are followed carefully. However, the publishers and authors disclaim all liability in connection with the use of the information in this book. If you have any doubts as to the suitability of the exercises in individual cases, please check with your doctor first.

Poem on page 26 adapted from the book *Children Learn What They Live* © 1998 by Dorothy Law Nolte and Rachel Harris, Workman Publishing Co. Inc., New York

Managing editor: Sarah Levete
Layout by: Neil Hawkins, ndesign
Cover design by: Neil Hawkins, ndesign
Illustrations by: Rebecca Rainbow

Printed in Great Britain by MPG Books Ltd, Bodmin, Cornwall

Contents

Chapter 6 Warm-ups and poses continued

Chapter 6 Warm-ups and poses

Chapter 6 Warm-ups and poses continued

The Authors

Three authors planned, researched and wrote *Helping Children with Yoga*.

Michelle Cheesbrough

Michelle trains teachers to teach yoga to children through the British Wheel of Yoga Children's Module. She also runs yoga classes for all age groups including parents with their toddlers. As a Registered General Nurse, the main emphasis of her work is health education through the practice of yoga.

Sarah Woodhouse

Sarah is Chief Executive of the Right from the Start education project and an experienced teacher, researcher and author.

Rosemary Griffiths

Rosemary specialized in Art and Divinity at Kirby Fields Training College. She taught first in a Froebel Kindergarten, then, for 12 years, in a primary school on Merseyside. She spent seven years studying yoga in a Christian Ashram in India run in the Indian tradition. Returning to the UK she taught Iyengar yoga practice to 7–11 year olds in a Birkenhead primary school.

Acknowledgements

The authors are grateful to those who contributed their ideas, experiences and knowledge to this book; especially to

Marguerite Smithwhite who taught yoga, meditation and art to primary school children in India, across Europe and in four London primary schools after her retirement.

Micheline Flak who is an international consultant on yoga in school. She launched RYE (Research on Yoga in Education) in Paris in 1978 and is now President. Through Micheline Flak, RYE was launched in the UK in 2005.

Rajiv and Swati Chanchani who have taught yoga to children in North India for many years and have generously given valuable advice and support.

Vedantanana Saraswati who is a Satyananda teacher and developed the British Wheel of Yoga module. This module is a course specially for training qualified yoga teachers to work with children. She has trained six teachers around the UK to continue with this work.

The authors would also like to express their warmest gratitude to Rebecca Rainbow for her beautiful drawings done directly from photographs of children in Rosemary's school, in Michelle's classes and in India, and for the tree drawing of her own child. The photographs were taken by Michelle Cheesbrough, Rosemary Griffiths, Keiron Tovell, Nick Butcher and Siemon Scamell-Katz. The children pictured in the illustrations and some of the photographs are Imogen, Jenny, Delphine, Philip, David, Alice, Claire, Shyam, Louise, Yolande, Lindsey, Anna, Mat, Emma, Sarah Jane, Alicia, Nicola, Freddy, Nell, Joanne, Beg, Patrick, Phoebe, Georgie, Leila and Claudia. Many thanks as well to the other children featured in the photographs.

The cover photograph taken by Keiron Tovell is of Phoebe and Georgie.

The photograph of Yehudi Menuhin was taken by Virginia Schmidt.

Thanks to Marshall Tyler for the use of his photographs on pages 32 and 38, taken at the Yoga Gallery, Winston-Salem, NC, USA (www.yogagallery.net).

We also thank Elaine Powell, a British Wheel of Yoga tutor, for permission to use the Flamingo Sequence which she devised.

Our thanks to all the children involved in the illustrations.

Finally, thanks to Sarah Levete for editing this book and to Neil Hawkins for his design.

There are numerous 'schools' of yoga which practise and teach the ancient tradition of yoga, each with its special area of emphasis and own style of teaching. The authors are grateful to the following established Schools of Yoga for valuable information and instruction: The British Wheel of Yoga, Satyananda and Iyengar.

Father and daughter balance in Tree Pose

Steady trees

Foreword

By Sir Yehudi Menuhin

Yehudi Menuhin was one of the best known, best loved and inspiring violinists ever known. He saw music and yoga as two great healing agents. He said that his own daily practice helped him to counterbalance the physical stress of playing the violin for hours every day from his childhood. He gave encouragement and valuable advice while this book was in preparation, and wrote this Foreword shortly before he died.

From my own experience, I can recommend the practice of Yoga with all my heart. It reaches our innermost parts and furthers our well-being. It deepens the breath, strengthens the heart, relaxes the body, co-ordinates our movements and lightens our step. It steadies our spirit.

It is my fervent hope that this beautifully prepared book about teaching yoga practice to children will be taken up by teachers, by parents and by leaders of children's clubs, and used widely and well.

They will find in it nothing but inspiration, satisfaction and an abiding source of energy and calm both for their own lives as well as for the children with whom they share it.

I can see how particularly valuable it will be for those many overactive or out-of-control or anxious and lonely children that there are in every class and in many of our homes.

The presentation of this book is imaginative in ways entirely appropriate to childhood – that transitory stage of human development. It will make a beautiful and enticing introduction to one of the world's most perfectly crafted disciplines.

Yehudi Menuhin

Three bows shooting together

Introduction

Yoga is perfect for children. Younger children enjoy making fun animal shapes and older children enjoy the flow and challenge of yoga poses. From turning the body into a bridge and paying full attention to colouring a mandala, yoga stretches body and mind. It engages children's natural sense of wonder and curiosity about themselves and their place in life.

Teaching yoga to children provides a steadying and harmonizing influence. It can balance hyperactive, lethargic or fidgety children. It can give all children more confidence, self-control and delight in themselves.

Yoga is an ideal activity to balance the physical and emotional needs of children, whether at school or at home. It both energizes and relaxes, making children more ready and open to learn. Practising yoga at home with children fosters a sense of togetherness and calm that spreads out into the rest of the day.

When children learn yoga, they hold a precious knowledge and understanding that they can draw on throughout the rest of their lives.

Right from the Start!

Helping Children with Yoga forms part of a series of books produced by **Right from the Start**, a charity working to reduce the present levels of stress, confusion and violence in childhood and to give children the best possible start in their lives.

The **Right from the Start** project responds to the growing need for a more balanced and healthy lifestyle, recognized in the UK government's Agenda for Healthy Schools. Its work is closely associated with the aims of other organizations set up to help parents and children, such as Home Start, Sure Start and the Parenting Education and Support Forum.

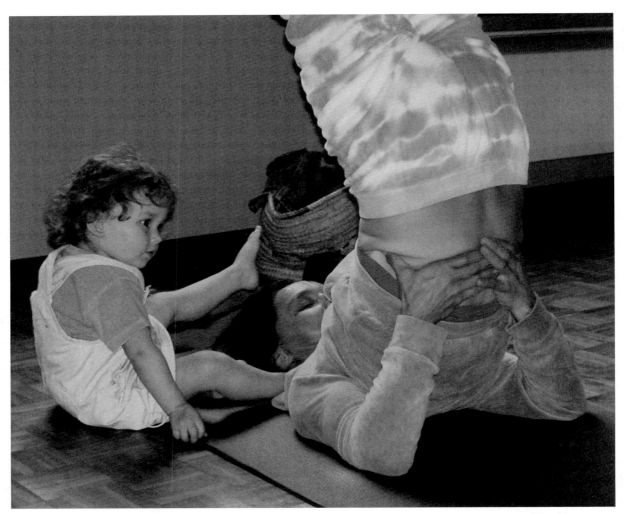

Watching mum

How to use this book

Helping Children with Yoga can inspire and guide your yoga practice with children. For people new to yoga, this book is a comprehensive introduction; for more experienced practitioners there are many imaginative suggestions to help you extend and develop children's yoga.

For everyone, this book helps you draw upon yoga to nurture and support children in their emotional and physical development.

The first section explores the philosophy that underpins yoga and discusses the benefits of yoga at home and at school. The second section provides clear instructions for different yoga poses, suitable for all levels of ability, and gives simple techniques for effective relaxation and meditation.

From quick, five-minute yoga energizers to introduce before any class, to enough poses for a full yoga session at home or school, this book provides a framework for integrating yoga into the lives of children.

All you need is a mat, the child and your imagination.

Explore and enjoy!

Safe Practice

Yoga practice, whether at home or at school, calls for thoughtfulness and care. If you are unsure about the suitability of any of the exercises, please check with a qualified health practitioner first. Before starting a posture, read the guidelines and instructions to check its suitability for the children in your care.

Teaching Yoga

The best and safest way to practise yoga is with a qualified teacher. Some teachers also specialize in yoga for children. You will find all the information you need on this in Appendix 2. Use this book to complement any yoga classes you or your child attends.

The authors recommend that parents do not teach yoga to other people's children unless they are suitably qualified. It is also essential for teachers to undertake training or to invite a qualified yoga teacher into the class.

Making animal shapes like the cow

Any questions?

Do I have to be bendy and very fit to do yoga with children?
No. You simply need a willingness to try and experiment.

Can any child do yoga?
Yoga is suitable for all levels of physical and intellectual ability. Many poses can be adapted to suit the physical needs of each child. Check with a qualified medical practitioner if you have doubts about the suitability of any of the postures or breathing exercises for a particular child.

Do I need special equipment?
No. For yoga poses, you need space for the children to stretch on and a non-slip mat.

What kind of yoga is best for children?
There are many schools or styles of yoga from Astanga to Iyengar. The style described and recommended here is Hatha. This includes postures, breathing, meditation and relaxation.

How long will it take?
A child obviously benefits more from a full session, and regular practice is what brings the rewards. However, you don't need to set aside a whole teaching session or an hour at home to benefit. The principles of yoga can be easily incorporated into everyday life; a child can still benefit from a fifteen-minute session of stretches, breathing and relaxation or perhaps a guided story or visualization (see pages 64 and 135).

I'm a primary school teacher. Do I need special qualifications to teach yoga?
See page 42 for some exercises and activities that you can use in a class without any training. Appendix 2 details the training opportunities available for teachers who wish to use yoga fully in their classes. Alternatively, you could invite a qualified children's yoga teacher to come and meet staff and discuss the possibilities for providing lessons. See pages 152–156 for details about how to contact a qualified teacher.

Is yoga about any particular religion?
Although yoga was developed by religious teachers in India, it is not now confined to any particular faith or religious practice. It is universal, building up children's inner spirit through increasing their self-confidence, self-control and giving them a sense of connectedness and peace. Yoga is for everyone to enjoy – and to discover the benefits.

My child has a physical disability. Can she do yoga?

Yes. It may be easy to adapt simple yoga poses to suit the physical needs of your child but you may need help and advice from a YOU & ME Yoga teacher or a YogaBuds teacher (see page 155).

At what age can a child start yoga?

A baby can do yoga (within limits!). Toddlers will copy their parents in everything, including yoga, as soon as they can move around. Contact Birthlight and the British Wheel of Yoga to find out about parent and toddler yoga classes in your area (see page 169).

Some postures such as headstand (see page 63) are not recommended for children younger than 12. Some breathing exercises are not suitable for children under eight.

Can a toddler concentrate long enough to do yoga?

Yoga for younger children (up until the age of about eight) is best supported by stories, games and music. Don't expect them to concentrate for more than a few moments. Just let them copy you and have fun together.

Fun and involvement from the beginning

SECTION ONE

HARMONY and BALANCE

*Yoga is for children who still know the
inner world and for others who seek
its rediscovery.*

Marguerite Smithwhite

Advanced poses such as Fish under the Bridge will challenge children

CHAPTER 1

What is yoga?

Yoga is a union of body and mind created through physical exercises, breathing techniques and relaxation, meditation and mindfulness.

The word 'yoga' comes from the ancient Sanskrit word meaning 'union' or 'wholeness'. This reminds us that the different parts of ourselves – body, emotions, mind and spirit – can be so well balanced that we can feel at one with our world, not separated from it,

Many people discover yoga through a desire for exercise and fitness. Yoga poses, also called postures, do indeed stretch the body. But many people come to discover that yoga also stretches the mind and inspires a journey of inner discovery.

When we understand and use the disciplines of yoga practice, we begin to feel at one with ourselves, with others and with the world around us.

Yoga Values
Yoga is an ancient art and science, built up over thousands of years by generations of wise men in India. These 'yogis' or 'rishis' – sages and saints – lived very close to nature. Truth, non-violence, honesty, self-discipline and simplicity were the values on which they built their lives.

The yogis and rishis lived far away from any city, surrounded by nature. Everything fascinated them: the glittering stars, the craggy mountains of the Himalayas, the fierce beasts, the flowing rivers, the beautiful birds, the delicate leaves, the darting fish, the floating lilies, even the ants and grasshoppers. From watching nature so closely, they developed a whole jungle of animal and bird yoga postures. They worked out systems and principles of how to live their lives very simply and harmoniously and developed their own special strength and control.

Around 300bc, one of these wise men, called Patanjali, brought together these principles into a set of values now called 'Patanjali's Eightfold Path'. This ancient code still typifies the essence of yoga and is the basis for most of the yoga practised today.

According to legend, a young woman called Gonika was bathing in the river one morning and she prayed to the Sun god as it rose up in the sky. "O lord, please grant me a glorious son!" Then the Sun god told the wise snake Shesha to be born again as Gonika's son. Shesha was a huge snake but immediately became tiny and dropped into Gonika's palms as she prayed, and changed himself into a beautiful baby boy. Gonika was full of joy and named the baby Pata-anjali. In Sanskrit, pata means 'falling' and anjali means 'palms folded in prayer'. Patanjali grew up to be an extraordinary man, famous for his knowledge, his understanding, his wisdom and his writings.

Patanjali's Eightfold Path

Patanjali's path lays down fundamental human values for behaviour that encourages sensitivity, understanding and co-operation. This code reminds us to encourage children's positive behaviour rather than being quick to reprimand children for behaviour we don't like.

The names used here are the original Sanskrit words for the different steps of this personal journey.

Yamas – values or personal attitudes for all people to cultivate
The five yamas are:

ahimsa – non violence
satya – truthfulness
asteya – honesty
brahmacharya – moderation and self-control
aparigraha – generosity

See Appendix 1 for a full exploration of the yamas

Niyamas – healthy and productive habits to develop
The five niyamas are:

saucha – purity
santosha – contentment
tapas – self-discipline
svadhyaya – self-observation and self-study
ishwarapranidhana – finding a sense of divinity

See Appendix 1 for a full exploration of the niyamas

Asanas – yoga exercises to balance and strengthen the body
The asanas are covered in detail on pages 74–124.

Pranayama – breathing exercises to cleanse and revitalize our bodies and minds
Breathing exercises are covered in detail on pages 125–132.

The final four steps on Patanjali's Eightfold Path describe how to find peace and calm and to meditate.

Pratyahara – calming and stilling the senses for a deep peace
(see the centring exercises for relaxation pages 134–136).

Dharana – increasing concentration by focusing full attention

Dhyana – the practice of meditation
Suggestions for meditation are given on pages 137–140.

Samadhi – touching the divine
See Appendix 1 for a full exploration of the final four stages of Patanjali's Eightfold Path.

Do I need to talk about niyamas and yamas to teach yoga to children?
It depends on you. Reading more about aspects of Patanjali's Eightfold Path (see Appendix 1) may help you formulate your thoughts about this. Some people will feel comfortable using terms such as niyamas and yamas; some may prefer to focus simply on the thoughts behind them. There is no right or wrong, only what feels most appropriate for you and for each child.

Patanjali's Eightfold Path shown as the branches of a tree

Talk to children about your own efforts to follow the yamas and niyamas and about your mistakes – remind them that what really matters is to be mindful and try again.

For a full discussion of yamas and niyamas see Appendix 1, pages 147–151.

Which yamas and niyamas might you select to be an inspiration for yourself, for your children and for your children's children? Do you need to adapt them at all? Ask your children or your class which ones feel most important to them? Why?

Alternatively, it can be intriguing to encourage children to draw a picture of their perception of the opposite of a yama or niyama. This can encourage children to reflect more clearly on what the values mean to them in their lives.

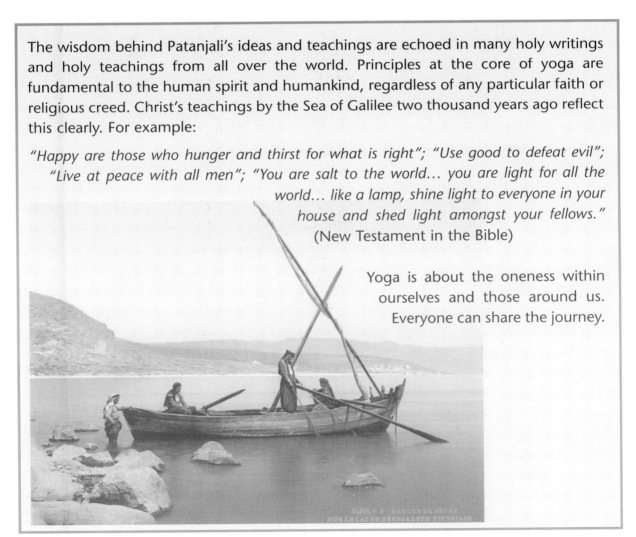

The wisdom behind Patanjali's ideas and teachings are echoed in many holy writings and holy teachings from all over the world. Principles at the core of yoga are fundamental to the human spirit and humankind, regardless of any particular faith or religious creed. Christ's teachings by the Sea of Galilee two thousand years ago reflect this clearly. For example:

"Happy are those who hunger and thirst for what is right"; "Use good to defeat evil"; "Live at peace with all men"; "You are salt to the world... you are light for all the world... like a lamp, shine light to everyone in your house and shed light amongst your fellows."
(New Testament in the Bible)

Yoga is about the oneness within ourselves and those around us. Everyone can share the journey.

Children Learn What They Live

If children live with criticism, they learn to condemn.

If children live with hostility, they learn to fight.

If children live with ridicule, they learn to feel shy.

If children live with shame, they learn to feel guilty.

If children live with encouragement, they learn confidence.

If children live with tolerance, they learn patience.

If children live with praise, they learn appreciation.

If children live with acceptance, they learn to love.

If children live with approval, they learn to like themselves.

If children live with honesty, they learn truthfulness.

If children live with security, they learn to have faith in themselves and in those about them.

If children live with friendliness, they learn the world is a nice place in which to live.

Dorothy Law Nolte

Our own yoga practice may help us discover the qualities we would like to pass on to our children.

Children respond to loving attention. Your awareness of yogic practice and philosophy will encourage a positive and nurturing care of children.

'Dog' in the garden!

Children support each other in partner poses, such as Friendship Tree

CHAPTER 2

Why teach yoga to children?

It works brilliantly and they love it!

Primary teacher

One of the best ways to establish a child's emotional harmony, and to help body, mind and spirit to mature together, is to teach children yoga and to help them enjoy it enough to want to continue practising.

Regular yoga practice can improve children's....

- physical strength, stamina and co-ordination
- posture and balance
- behaviour
- schoolwork.

With regular yoga practice...

- children will have warmer and easier relationships with family, teachers and friends.
- hyperactive and disruptive children will grow calmer, particularly through the practice of breathing techniques.
- anxious children will become more outgoing and confident.
- children will find it easier to remember what they have been taught.

Yoga gives children an interest and a sense of challenge. Through better understanding and care of themselves they learn tolerance towards others. Learning to breathe correctly, to relax at will, to bring the art of concentration into work and play and keep the body supple and strong will improve the quality of a child's life – both at home and at school.

Strong and steady like a warrior

A Balanced Life

Yoga is interesting as it makes you think how you live.

12 year old

Our children are often pushed into a struggle to achieve in every area of their lives. They often long to possess more than they truly need or want, through the commercial pressures on them and on their parents, and the emotional pressure of keeping up with their friends. The very nature of yoga teaching involves respect for the uniqueness of every person. It is about accepting ourselves, not about measuring up to outside standards. Yoga gives children space to explore themselves and to be themselves, without having to compete.

More time is needed for the natural instinctive exercise children take when they play outside – running, chasing, jumping, balancing, climbing, crawling, rolling and laughing. In schools, PE and sports, such as football, provide children with essential physical exercise. Yoga differs from these types of exercise because it is non-competitive and harmonizes both body and mind. This can have a significant impact upon a child's ability and willingness to learn in all fields.

The benefits from yoga will help to bring out the very best in children if they practise regularly and are reminded of the techniques until these have been integrated into their lives. The pleasure and confidence that comes from practising balance and control of the body and mind allows children's personalities to flower with a new awareness and appreciation of themselves and kindness for others. It helps them to feel glad about themselves, the first step towards loving life, other people and the marvels and beauty in creation.

Feeling Good

Good self-esteem makes children feel happy and in control. This can shine in them like gold. A child may have highs and lows in any area: physical, social, emotional and intellectual. The challenge is to notice where a child's self-esteem is high and where it falters or is low. For example, a child's self-esteem can be high in one area – perhaps football or biking or dancing and show as a joyful showing-off of physical ability and control. At another level, the same child may have low self-esteem, perhaps becoming shy, awkward and monosyllabic in certain social situations. Good self-esteem enables a child to cope with difficult situations without being overtaken by frustration or anger, and to reach out to others to give support and comfort.

Jump for joy!

Strong intellectual self-esteem shows in the positive way children approach schoolwork and their curiosity about the world beyond themselves as they meet it, learning everything they can. The practice of yoga, combining balanced physical exercise and awareness of the mind, can enhance a child's overall self-esteem.

The Whole Person

Yoga is a holistic discipline, about the whole person. The postures make us strong and supple but the movements help to balance our bodies by massaging our glands and internal organs. This can help release tension, and calm and clear the mind. This enhances learning and concentration.

Kids with Attention Deficit Hyperactivity Disorder (ADHD) crave movement. Yoga can slow down and channel these impulses and it can also instil a peacefulness and calmness – something every parent craves.

Françoise Freedman, Founder and Director of Birthlight, yoga teacher and author

Yoga addresses the whole child from his or her physical development to emotional balance. It gives children a feeling of undivided care and attention and a sense of self-control and peace. Yoga makes our bodies strong and supple, our minds concentrated and calm, and it lifts our spirit.

Before practising yoga poses, breathing exercises and relaxation, it helps to have an image about the interlinking parts that make up a whole being. This image of a chariot may help you and some older children to visualize this wholeness. Children may or may not feel interested in discussing this. Let them choose the moment; then perhaps invite them to draw their own chariot, at the end of the discussion.

Group concentration

Imagine yourself as a chariot pulled by prancing horses, and understand how the four parts of yourself need to work together well, or life may gallop out of control!

The chariot is your body.
The horses are your senses and emotions.
The reins are your mind.
The driver, holding the reins, is your inner spirit or self.

The driver controls the galloping horses to find the right road for your journey through life.
Yoga can help you to harness and drive the horses and chariot safely and well.

Now we can think about each part – our body, our mind, our feelings, our spirit; and how
yoga can help us find the best in each of them.

The Body and Yoga

Understanding the make-up of the human body can help older children appreciate the links
between body and mind:

> the skeleton – the framework of bones which supports us, especially our spine –
> our backbone;
>
> the muscles which move us;
>
> the nerves which carry messages from our brain to and from each part of our body.

Our lungs, circulation and digestive processes bring oxygen to cleanse and recharge our
muscles and deliver the nourishment from our food to where it is needed.

Relaxing in Lying Twist

Yoga will stretch every part of the spine, helping to make it strong and flexible and keeping it in good condition for life. Stretching the spine stretches the spinal cord and frees the nerves from any pressures. Nerves send messages throughout the body, like telephone wires that pass up and down through the spinal cord, inside our backbone. Yoga's attention to correct posture can positively affect many aspects of our health.

All the glands around our body – the endocrine system – form an important working team. They are like tiny factories that work to keep the chemicals (hormones) in our bodies balanced so that we are healthy and feel at ease.

Hormones relate directly to emotions. Stress causes the adrenal glands to become overactive. Yoga postures help our glands to work together efficiently. The gentle pressure that the stretching and bending of yoga postures puts on internal organs keeps the glands in balance and we begin to feel better and calmer.

The Mind and Yoga

Mind is the thinking part of ourselves. It can notice everything around us, have ideas, imagine and learn. It can look ahead to the future and remember things that have already happened to us. With our minds, we explore new ways, new facts and new possibilities. We discover why we are like we are and what we can become. Yoga helps us to think things through.

The Emotions and Yoga

When we are young, our brains grow rapidly and make new connections all the time. More often than not, our emotions lead us. We live through the many different feelings which surge up in us in quick succession, often suddenly and sometimes strongly. As we grow older, we become more able to make sense of our feelings; to use our minds to think through our experiences and respond more sensibly and thoughtfully.

The Self and Yoga

We all have in us a hidden treasure that we can call our 'spirit', 'soul' or 'self'. Yoga helps us to unlock this spiritual part of ourselves and know it better.

Our personality shows as a blend of our mind, our emotions and our spirit, working together.

Understanding Emotions

I can tell what I am feeling now. I like that.

Patti, aged 9

It is important for children to identify and name the huge range of emotions they may feel. Yoga can help towards this by encouraging an awareness of the body and a focus on the mind. This can help children to recognize where they feel certain emotions in their bodies. For example, some of us feel fear in our stomach, grief in our throat and anger in our jaw and head. Some may also feel love and compassion in the throat or the chest. Once a child is able to identify an overwhelming emotion and name and place it, the feeling becomes easier to accept and then control.

Yoga practice can lead children inwards towards a state of thoughtfulness and meditation. When children learn to meditate through yoga, they will become increasingly in tune with their emotional lives and better able to understand and talk about their feelings. David Fontana and Ingrid Slack's book, *Teaching Meditation to Children*, describes meditation exercises to help children experience fear, anger and sadness very imaginatively and to look at them in a way which will help them to understand and handle these feelings more easily.

Different yoga postures can help address the varied emotional needs of a child. For instance,
- Boat (see page 83) and Hare (see page 98) have a calming and relaxing effect
- The Magic Five Breaths Technique (see page 132) helps reduce stress, anxiety and fear
- Volcano (see page 132) helps a child deal with anger.

The best is the relaxation because it calms me when I am feeling bad or nervous.

Thiery, aged 9

Child Pose calms and relaxes

CHAPTER 3

Yoga and learning

The most important part of our school curriculum is the yoga and meditation the children do each day. The effect it has on all their school work, their contentment and the way they relate to each other and the staff is extraordinary. Many of the children come from very deprived backgrounds.

Teacher, Parenting Project USA

Yoga in school enhances learning. Because yoga is able to bring to children such an improvement in the quality of their attention and concentration, it can lead them straight to the discovery or rediscovery of real joy in learning.

Talking of yoga in school or just of yoga for children would have appeared revolutionary 40 years ago. However, the pioneering research and work of Micheline Flak who set up RYE (Research on Yoga in Education) in the 1970s in Paris is now spreading worldwide. The success of her work with children is now reflected in the experience of teachers in many countries who have followed her techniques.

Yoga within Education

Yoga is all about physical and mental balance and harmony. Over the past decade there have been profound discoveries about the brain, particularly through the use of magnetic resonance imaging (MRI). Neuroscience has provided breakthrough knowledge about brain development and how children learn. These discoveries about how the brain works have infused new passion into the political debate about education and current teaching methods.

Because yoga helps children to use the whole brain, more and more people are being trained to teach yoga to children. This will be a great help to class teachers who are showing an increasing interest in using the stress-releasing techniques that yoga can offer because it is so widely recognized that children can neither learn nor feel happy if they are stressed. Current teaching methods need to change and are beginning to do so.

'Kerry has calmed down a lot in her behaviour since beginning yoga.'

Secondary teacher

PSHE (personal and social health education) helps to address the social aspects of life such as growing concerns about healthy eating, conflict resolution, emotional intelligence, the prevention of bullying and the introduction of initiatives such as mentoring schemes. Yoga provides an overarching system that supports PSHE.

Full attention

Concentration is when the mind is absorbed – giving undivided attention to something. Children often don't know what the word 'concentration' means or what it feels like to pay total attention to a single thing. For some children, this purposeful focus comes naturally but for others, being given tools to help them focus will be important.

Children's attention can be absorbed, uneven or slack. It changes according to various factors such as any recent activity, the child's diet and his/her current experiences and concerns at home and at school. Yoga is particularly valuable to children with poor concentration. It also adds a new depth of awareness and concentration to other children.

'I found that as children concentrate on the movements they are making, they definitely begin to develop a higher awareness.'

Primary teacher

Peaceful breathing

In yoga practice, children have to listen and stay alert to follow the instructions; they have to co-ordinate their movements with their breathing, sometimes counting the breath in a breathing exercise. Through these controlled yoga movements children learn self-control.

This can help them to respond in positive ways to whatever is going on. They are learning to be attentive, to be aware and to live in the present moment. Concentration improves with regular practice.

'The staff are so much less stressed since yoga became a recognized and regular part of the school programme. They see changes in the children's ability to concentrate and use their energy creatively in what they are meant to be doing!'

Primary headteacher

Yoga for Focus

The Restless Ones
Many children find it very hard to sit still at a table for long and become quickly fidgety and distracted. Physical restriction hurts and frequent movement is essential. To stretch and calm them, try:

- The Swaying Palm Tree (see page 76)
- Alternate Nostril Breathing (see page 130)
- Shoulder Lifts (see page 72).

The Wild Ones
These are children who are hyperactive, perhaps disruptive or out-of-control after games or playtime or on windy days. They may behave all week like it's Friday afternoon. To focus attention, try:

- The Woodchopper (see page 131)
- Hissing Balloon Breath (see page 130)
- the Tree and any of the other balance postures (see page 80).

The Monday Morning Ones
These are the more withdrawn and dreamy children. They may seem lethargic and easily feel tired – or too hot or too cold. They may benefit from:

- Staircase Breathing (see page 131)
- Simple neck exercises to carry more oxygen to the brain (see page 73)
- Blackboard Back – invite children, in pairs, to take turns to draw a shape or a number or a picture on the other child's back. When the 'blackboard' has guessed right, the artist wipes the board clean with his hands.

In general, a child's ability to concentrate is one and a half times the age of that child. For example, an eight year old should be able to concentrate continuously for a maximum of 12 minutes at a time. Less able children or children with attention deficit hyperactivity disorder (ADHD) obviously manage much less than this but will often respond well to yoga with a four to five minute break, with further breathing exercises and a movement game to refresh them.

Teachers who know their children well, quickly become able to assess the type of energy present in the whole group and grow confident in their choice of yoga postures which can work for everyone and draw the children together. Yoga can balance the energy of both the individual child and the class as a whole.

Self Belief

Everyone needs individual, loving attention. No wonder that genuine praise is like gold. For children, it is the best possible proof that the teacher is watching them, listening to them and recognizing their efforts. Yoga provides a way for teachers to build-up the self-esteem of every one of their children.

How happy and successful each child becomes will depend upon the beliefs that each holds about their own abilities.

Positive Thinking

Affirm each child daily with an individual smile, a word or another small gesture of appreciation. Point out the child's strengths and help positively in areas where the child is struggling – the response will often be dramatic.

The greatest benefit, I feel, has been for the children who are barely able to cope with difficult situations at home or in class. Yoga gives them a measure of confidence and an inner strength they did not know they had.

Secondary teacher

Positive Thoughts

Sankalpas are positive affirmations. They are words or phrases that are repeated at least three times in order to replace negative thinking patterns. Sankalpas are spoken silently. Here are some examples of phrases that can be written down for children to choose for themselves. Adapt the phrases and add new ones to suit each child.

Jump like a frog!

Some Sankalpas

I can stay calm when the going gets tough.

I'm a strong and brave person.

I'm happy to be me.

Today is going to be fine.

I'm a kind person.

I can try hard and I can do things well.

Our third daughter was severely dyslexic, failing at school and getting very upset about her homework. The turning point was when we got her standing in front of a full-length mirror each morning before she went to school, smiling at her reflection in the mirror and saying loudly and clearly, "I have a brilliant brain!!". From that day she began to grow more confident and happy despite all the struggles. She is a real success story.

Noël

41

Make your own 'angel cards' with simple, single words of affirmation on each. Everyone picks one out of the box and it becomes an affirmation for themselves. It works best if a child sticks with the same affirmation until he or she feels it is coming true. If one particular child seems to be struggling you might also decide to help by giving that child a sankalpa especially for him or herself.

Positive affirmation exercises can be done any time, anywhere, but they work very well at the beginning and again at the end of a yoga practice.

Introducing Yoga at School

In advance of, and in addition to yoga at school taught by a trained children's yoga teacher, any teacher who is already practising yoga can introduce children to these simple and useful exercises and activities:

- Warm-up sequence (see page 71).
- Mountain Pose (see page 75).
- Guided stories and visualization (see pages 66 and 135) – if you use 'The Cat in the Wood', invite the children to invent their own simple animal shapes to match the storyline – the proper postures should be taught by a trained teacher.
- Breathing exercises such as Blowing Feathers, Humming Bee Breath and Hissing Balloon Breath (see pages 128–130).

**As a primary school teacher I was amazed to discover how difficult young children found it to 'find' their breath. Asking a six year old to use breathing techniques to help manage frustration took quite a few minutes the first time – but once learned, children seem to recall the techniques with ease. For younger children, individually and in groups, breathing techniques work very effectively.

As far as older children are concerned, I have used yoga postures in English, through drama. Groups of children up to eight very much enjoy using yoga to warm up for expressive drama sessions. We also use sequences of postures to consolidate their learning, focus their concentration and bring awareness to their bodies for character expression.**

Suzi Phillips, Bungay Middle School

Learning Through The Senses

How we learn is just as important as what we learn. When you imagine a scene, do you see, hear, feel, taste or smell the image? Or do you use two or more senses in combination?

Children can remember and retain what they have learned when they have received information using as many of the senses as possible. It is worth finding out what kind of learner your child is.

We sense in multiple ways and we learn in multiple ways. Some of us respond most readily to sounds and the spoken word – these are mainly **auditory learners**. Some need to see or form a diagram or picture to understand an idea – these are predominantly **visual learners**. Others learn things through their bodies – these are mainly **kinesthetic learners**. Most of us respond in all these ways but one way or more will be dominant. Awareness of a child's preferred learning style can help you provide strategies to enhance the child's learning. Children's confidence and ability will rise steadily if they are helped to learn in ways that suit them.

Knowing this and watching out for these differences helps teachers to structure their yoga lessons successfully. They will be alert to the children's multiple ways of sensing and learning. They will recognize what becomes 'favourite' to each child, understand the reason why and respect it.

Visual learners will particularly enjoy the guided imagery parts of the lesson and may like to keep a drawing journal of postures as they learn them. Videos and details in colourful books about yoga will delight them and they will remember what they have seen. They will enjoy colouring mandalas (see pages 158–160).

Colouring mandalas appeals especially to visual learners

Auditory learners will enjoy doing yoga to music and also singing. They will be good at listening to a story during relaxation. They will enjoy listening to the instructions for each pose.

Kinesthetic learners will like to invent yoga postures and work on group postures. These learners prefer doing a wide range of yoga postures with their bodies rather than thinking about them.

Whole Brain Learning

The brain is two-sided and needs to be in balance. Each side processes particular kinds of information and is responsible for different kinds of thinking and working. The left brain controls the right side of the body. The right brain controls the left side of the body. Girls, as a whole, tend more towards right-brain dominance and boys towards left-brain dominance.

Some children tend to become primarily left-brain learners and others primarily right-brain learners. The left-brain hemisphere and right-brain hemisphere need to work together in balance. A marked imbalance and lack of communication between left and right hemispheres can place a child at a disadvantage: he or she will be less sensitive to others and less competent in their daily life by not using both sides in harmony.

Most of the present educational systems push children into a left-brain way of working. This means that the balance has been lost for many children and needs to be recovered. The practice of yoga and the use of such skills as Brain Gym® and accelerated learning (see pages 169, 170 for further information on these techniques) are proving to be invaluable towards this end. They are able to make a very great difference to children's behaviour, their relationships with their teachers, families and friends and their ability to learn.

Due to the recent surge of brain science studies, there has been a leap in our understanding of individual learning styles. Research into what can best help each child use and integrate both sides of the brain is proving to be vital for children's happiness, confidence and ability to learn and remember.

Yoga, and other brain-based learning techniques such as accelerated learning, all involve using both sides of the brain. These techniques can be very helpful to children whose brains are still growing rapidly. They are equally helpful in rebalancing an adult brain which may have got itself into a rut. All these techniques can help everyone towards achieving his or her full learning potential.

A thorough yoga class will contain a kinesthetic, auditory and visual component and build the vital link between the two sides of the brain.

Left-brain users are drawn towards:	Right-brain users are drawn towards:
Logic	Imagination, pictures, metaphors
Language	Ideas
Writing	Daydreams, insight, intuition
Numbers	Rhyming
Spelling	Music and rhythm
Reading	Sport
Factual information	Space-oriented tasks
Methodical and time-oriented tasks	Three-dimensional images, patterns, connections
Step-by-step processes	
Getting the details right	Bringing everything together for understanding

Children whose areas of strength are from the right brain may get caught up in philosophical concepts and the story or development of a story. The mainly left-brained child will want the proof of a logical explanation. The latter may enjoy the challenge of creating a geometrical design for a mandala but the mainly right-brained child will become more absorbed in the colouring and sense of self found in the completed picture.

Experiences of a yoga teacher

Michelle Cheesbrough describes here how she became involved first in teaching yoga to children and then running courses to train teachers and parents to do the same. She was a nurse for 18 years and then taught yoga to adults and children full-time. Because of her particular interest in holistic care and concern about stress-related illness, she came to believe that working with children was the way forward. She describes her journey.

❝I watched my daughter Rosa's enjoyment and curiosity about yoga and it was this which led me into teaching children. I completed the British Wheel of Yoga Diploma course and began teaching adults. Introducing my daughter to yoga made me realize that, through the practice of yoga, children can learn to develop a healthy lifestyle. They will learn that health and healing is primarily in their own hands. When this can happen, they will feel less helpless and have a more positive outlook to help them to cope well when they are ill.

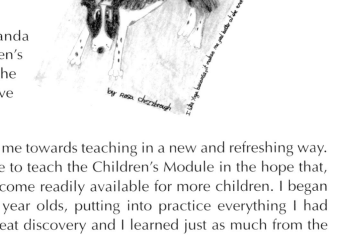

by Rosa Chezzbrough

When I did the yoga training course I had no idea how important this work would become to me. Teaching yoga to children and training parents and teachers to teach yoga to children has now become my passion and my primary work.

I trained through Swami Vedantananda Saraswati's British Wheel of Yoga Children's Module. I was inspired by the content of the course and how it was delivered. I have continued to develop this module.

The Diploma course opened the doors for me towards teaching in a new and refreshing way. I then trained along with five other people to teach the Children's Module in the hope that, after training more teachers, yoga will become readily available for more children. I began teaching an after-school group for 6–10 year olds, putting into practice everything I had learned on the course. It was a year of great discovery and I learned just as much from the children as I had from the course. The value of light-hearted yoga for children became obvious to me so quickly.

During the next few years, I taught other groups of children, also Brownies, Guides, children with special educational needs, a PE class in Middle School and pupils in a High School to relieve exam stress. I also teach three private classes, each of them very different in approach to match the different stages in the children's development. These three groups are called, '**Dragonflies**', '**Monkeys**' and '**Eagles**'.

Dragonflies is a parent and toddler group. Parents and children practise yoga together. This class encourages play, song and rhyming while exploring simple movements and animal postures in the context of the natural world. The toddlers imitate their parents who may help them with gentle movements. Some lovely bonding moments follow from this interaction. The toddlers love imaginative play with repetition of favourite songs and movement. They are exploring and learning about the world through their senses.

> Hester, Lois' mother, describes Lois' response to Michelle's parent and toddler group.
>
> *When we first started our Yoga Class I wasn't sure how much of it would sink in. Lois was only nine months old. Michelle was quite positive that the babies and toddlers were taking it all in at their own pace and that, one day in the future, we'd all be amazed at their ability.*
>
> *A year or so later, that day came. I was playing with Lois in her room before bed and I suggested we did some yoga. We sat down on the floor and I asked her what posture she wanted to do. "The Cow", she said at once. Astonished I watched on as she drew in a breath and put one arm behind her back and the other above her head, nearly linked her fingers and mooed. Quite sophisticated I thought.*
>
> *Without much encouragement we worked through her repertoire: snake, cat, dog, tree, frog, tortoise, buzzy bee breath, bridge, swan, lion. We are working on the warrior.*
>
> *I was so chuffed. It is great to be able to share yoga with her. We both get to see our friends, stretch out the tension and relax and it really is sinking in. We both love Wednesdays.*

Monkeys is for 7–13 year olds. This is a great age to learn good techniques in yoga postures, as the children are becoming stronger and more agile. This is a good time to use a lesson with a theme or story and plenty of games. Friendships have greater significance as a lot of emotional development is taking place.

Two teenage 'Eagles' making the shape of the Moon

This is why I like to use Jenny Mosley's circle time with this group (see Resources, page 170). It works really well. Circle time can happen at school or around the kitchen table or during a cooking or gardening activity at home or even during a journey. It can provide a good time to talk about yamas and niyamas in the context of what has been going on that day.

Eagles is a group of 13–16 year olds. These teenagers enjoy more challenging poses and the pupils can make up sequences of their own. They are also capable of longer periods of concentration and enjoy exploring some philosophical and abstract ideas such as peace, freedom and conflict. Teaching stress management is invaluable to young people as they move towards exam time and perhaps face adolescent difficulties at home.

A partner pose challenge

Play, games, stories, creative art and music are the cornerstones of teaching yoga to children, making yoga sessions imaginative and interactive. Non-competitive games are lots of fun and teach the children how to co-operate and help each other. They allow the children to let off steam so they become quiet and ready for a yoga session.

I have found teaching children both rewarding and challenging. The trick is to be aware of the energy in the group and to harness that energy in ways which draw together the children's focus of attention. This may mean dropping some of the ideas from your lesson plan and becoming more spontaneous through awareness of the children's needs for that day. Stillness is introduced for short periods in among other activities. A typical yoga session will be a mixture of movement and stillness. Most children enjoy the relaxation at the end of each session and some children will ask for it at the beginning. There is nothing quite like the calm atmosphere when they come out of relaxation and colour in a mandala or draw in their journals, chatting quietly and chewing on dried fruit.

we will miss you a lot. will you please come back. I hake you sor teaching us. I will still remember your yoga lessons. I will never sor get you and I will never sor get your music

Robert

Thank you very much for our amazing yoga lessons. I reckon it was great I like all of the yoga postures and I like it when you hav to do team work.

Jai

I like the blowing the feathers with straws and the postures where good too so was the adventures my favourite Adventures was the Sun. I really enjoyed it because it was relaxing.

Christina

I love the snake posture because it stretched my back. I liked the relaxation at the end of each session. It relaxed all my bones in my body.

Ashley

I am touched by these comments and notice too how these children are infusing little bits of yoga into their lives, being aware enough to take charge when things go out of balance. Some children use yoga to help them get to sleep. Some have taught their friends and families how to relax. Others have used breathing techniques at school during moments of stress. As a teacher I cannot ask for more than that. 🗨

Lesley Douglas from Beccles Middle School in Suffolk describes the effect of Michelle's work with her group of children with special needs.

The children I teach have various learning difficulties ranging from moderate learning difficulties, speech and language problems, communication disorders, behaviour problems, cerebral palsy, ADHD and autism. Michelle's yoga course with them has been amazingly beneficial for the children concerned. Initially the children were very excited and this was very difficult to manage. The difference over the weeks has been remarkable. Lots of the children have told me they use some of the techniques at home to help them with feelings of anger and frustration and their sleeplessness.

CHAPTER 4

Yoga at home

Parents who have attended a yoga class and are practising at home can teach yoga to their own children. They know their own children well and can rely on this and their own experience and commonsense. They are responsible for their own children's safety.

> Sit quietly somewhere comfortable with your eyes closed and begin to breathe slowly and easily. Visualize yourself being warm and patient with your child as you would like to be, just enjoying each other. This can be repeated again and again and can be especially useful whenever you want to feel closer to your child.

Closeness and Trust
Practising yoga with your child is a wonderful bonding experience, with endless opportunities for touch, smiles, talk and play. Children of three or older delight more and more in their ability to make unusual shapes with their bodies and to copy the sounds of nature, such as animals, flowing water or the wind in the trees. Suggest whatever else inspires you!

Centring
Spend a minute if you can with your toddler and up to three minutes with an older child just sitting quietly together listening to your own breathing. This is called centring and it prepares your mind for yoga.

Listening to your Voice
The soothing sounds of your voice carry your love for your children. This nourishes them and deepens your connection to each other. At the quiet beginning or ending of your yoga together you may decide to read a poem, a short story or say an affirmation or your own prayer – like a kind of favourite family message for yourselves.

Closeness and trust

Start Simply

Start simply with any yoga exercises you are familiar and comfortable with. Otherwise, choose some of the easier asanas (marked by ✿). As you practise, your child will naturally want to mimic what you are doing. A toddler will probably crawl all over you in great delight. An older child will instinctively want to join in, particularly given the chance to tumble about on the floor.

A family of snakes

Go with the Flow

There will be some days when your toddler is busy doing something else and an older child is not interested in practising with you. Before you start doing yoga together just check how your child is feeling about it. How does he react to a positive invitation to join in? If he is resolutely uninterested, carry on with your own practice. Allow him to come and go, without any pressure. When a child does join in, always show your pleasure in the sharing and in the child's efforts and achievements.

Quiet Time!

The television needs to be switched off during yoga practice to ensure a calm atmosphere. Even if your child is not practising with you, she needs to understand your need for peace. Give her toys instead to play with nearby. Older children may like to draw or colour in a mandala. They will still be within the atmosphere of the yoga space.

Relax!

'I couldn't sleep and so I did "Peaceful Places" and now I sleep much better.'

If you find your children become a bit restless during relaxation it can help a lot if you use gentle massage on their hands, feet or forehead. As soon as they get used to your doing this, they just love it.

The Spaghetti Test (see page 134) works really well for a child who is only just beginning to learn how to relax at will.

What Time?

'I get dressed as quickly as I can in the morning so I can do my yoga.'

Aged 10

The ideal time for yoga is early morning but this is probably not ideal for most families! If your child wakes early and you are not yet into the flurry of preparations for the day, you can do yoga together before breakfast or any time an hour after you have eaten. If early yoga doesn't fit in with your routine, find a slot in the day that suits you – preferably more or less at the same time each day.

Morning yoga is a wonderful way of gathering yourself together after sleep and getting ready for the day. It can be energetic and fun, with music to help bring all the senses alive. As well as talking about the yoga postures you share together, it helps children to listen to you talking about the rhythm of the day and what is going to happen between now and bedtime, especially if there might be differences to the normal routine.

Alternatively, you may decide to do yoga together in the evening as a wind-down towards bedtime. Dim the lights and use a soft blanket or 'fleece' for you and your child to lie on for the lying down poses and to lie underneath for relaxation.

Getting the Room Ready

If you have only minimal floor space at home, you may need to create enough room by shifting the furniture a little. All you need is space enough to lie down with arms and legs stretched out like two starfish.

Our flat is very small and the living room is choc-a-bloc but our entrance hall is wide and long enough for the two of us to stretch out so that's where we go. It works fine.

A grandfather

Yoga outside, in the fresh air in summer time, is even better. Best of all is yoga outside on the grass, underneath a tree, and being able to look up through the leaves.

Garden yoga

Story Time

Sometimes it may just be appropriate to share a story with your child and use it to guide you towards some fun yoga postures. See pages 66–68 for stories to inspire you.

Other Resources

DVDs and videos on yoga for children can be helpful especially when you are at the starting stage. See resources section for details of books and DVDs.

Enjoying a yoga book
about animals

Evie loves her yoga group. It has given her a wonderful sense of herself. Our teacher introduced us to the Yoga Kids DVD which we play at home. Evie delighted in watching the other children in the group doing yoga and now enjoys every opportunity to practise her yoga at home using the DVD. It's brilliant!

Liza

Yoga Classes

Parents may decide that it's well worthwhile searching locally to find a trained yoga teacher who has experience in teaching yoga to children. This support can be invaluable as your children grow older, especially if there is no plan to introduce yoga at their school. Perhaps you will want to get together with other parents and do something to encourage this to happen? See page 153 for details on how to find out about yoga classes in your area.

Doing yoga at home helps children in all kinds of ways when they go to school. Among other things it can help them to work without fear of failure.

SECTION TWO

YOGA in ACTION

Yoga is something that every child should be taught as a life skill. It is a practice that enables them to understand and experience how their bodies and minds work and puts maintenance of their physical and mental wellbeing within their own control.

Dr Peter Davies, School of Integrated Health at the University of Westminster

Mum watches and helps

CHAPTER 5

Ready to go!

For toddlers and younger children, yoga practice mostly consists of copying movements and postures and of children getting the feel of their bodies and a good balance. Avoid putting too much stress on young joints by encouraging young children to hold postures for only a breath or two, and help them come in and out of postures rhythmically.

Four–eight year olds can start by holding a posture for one breath, gradually increasing to three breaths. Children over eight can slowly increase the time they hold a posture but this will depend on the child's regular yoga practice and capability.

Up to the ages of seven or eight, yoga needs really to be just informal games and stretching exercises with music. Yoga with children should be full of 'let's pretend' and stories (see pages 66–68 for some ideas).

Children's Flexibility

Children in the primary years are very vulnerable because bones, muscles and ligaments are growing in spurts (children's brains too!). Everyone's bones are slightly different, especially in the way they connect. No two children will 'feel' a posture in the same way even if they appear to be the same build.

With practice, everyone can increase their flexibility; muscles can stretch out and pull back and tension can be released, but only up to an individual point. This point comes when a child (or adult) reaches a state of compression – where bone meets bone or where tissue is compacted between bone and bone. When a child in a posture reaches a state of compression, no amount of stretching will help extend the posture. Parents and teachers need to recognize this so that children never feel pressurized or disappointed if they cannot do some of the more advanced postures.

SAFETY

Space
- The space needs to be clean, airy and free from clutter and distractions – no television on or fidgeting pet in the room.
- At school, follow the school's guidelines of safe practice as with PE (physical education).

Equipment
- Use a non-slip mat on a firm surface, preferably a yoga mat rather than an exercise mat that can be slippery. If the floor is carpeted, you will still need a yoga mat for the standing postures. Yoga mats are available in many department stores and supermarkets.
- You will need a light blanket for each child, to stay warm in relaxation.
- If using music, make sure the equipment is ready.
- If you use candles, make sure they are kept away from inquisitive children.

Getting ready!

It's not a Competition

Yoga should never be competitive nor a performance. Some children have a tendency to try and outdo each other. Resist this, and keep reminding them that yoga is not a competition but just for themselves alone. Discourage them from watching each other, so they are not trying to make comparisons.

It's all OK

Every movement towards any posture is positive, as long as it is safe. Children will always aim to improve and keep practising if they become interested. Different postures come more easily to one child than to another. Help the children recognize their own improvements as they go along. That's all that matters.

Easy or Difficult?

Each yoga posture is 'starred' ☆ for its level of ease or challenge, from one star (simple postures) to three stars (challenging postures). Start with easier postures. As you and the children gain in confidence and physical ease, carefully introduce other postures. Each posture described in this book also has a safety precaution added if necessary. Build up yoga practice slowly and gently – there's no rush!

Many triangles

Planning a Session

- Always begin with a warm-up.

- Start with simple postures and progress to the more difficult ones. When choosing postures, take into account the physical aptitude of the children you are teaching.

- Early morning for yoga is best but may not be possible. Choose a time when the children are not too tired, or for parents at home, yoga as part of together-time before bedtime may be perfect. Choose postures that energize when children are lethargic or calming when you need them to quieten!

- Read the instructions for each posture before suggesting it, being aware of its suitability for the children you are teaching.

- Use a mixture of postures from the different groups such as forward bending postures balanced with back bending postures, standing with sitting postures and so on.

- Always counterbalance back bends with forward bends.

- Introduce new postures all the time so no one gets bored.

- End each session with the relaxation posture (see page 112) or an extended relaxation.

Keep an Eye!

During the session:

- Teach each child individually how to practise the postures slowly and deliberately. Teach them how to come out of a posture as well as going into the posture.

- Watch each child's face carefully for any signs of uncertainty.

- Nothing should hurt. Tell children to stop if it does.

- Move smoothly into a position. Jerking can place strain on children's joints.

- Toddlers should not hold a posture for longer than their instinct tells them, which is usually to move into a posture and straight out of it again. Respect this instinct.

- Make sure children keep breathing freely while they move into, hold and move out of a posture.

- Always check that the children are well before you begin, and check for any back problems. If they are not well or very tired, let them watch and just enjoy the relaxation exercises.

Headstands, Shoulderstands and Plough

You may perhaps be doing shoulderstands and headstands yourself at your yoga class or have a book or CD which includes instructions for these advanced postures.

The headstand is not included here. It is not safe for most children under 12 because the cranial bones may not yet have fully hardened and meshed before that age and the posture can put too much weight on a child's still-delicate neck bones and skull.

In order to do a headstand safely, a child needs to have enough strength in the upper body. To support the body weight through shoulders and arms, the child's arms need to be long enough; this means if the arm is bent and then the elbow raised to head level, the elbow must be level with or higher than the top of the skull.

Children who are overweight and neither flexible nor strong should never attempt headstands or even shoulderstands, whatever their age.

Shoulderstands (see page 104), like headstands, must be worked towards carefully and precisely over a period of time so that there will be a purposeful build-up of a child's strength and capability. The same principles apply for the Plough pose (see page 103).

However, this can still leave some parents and teachers with a dilemma simply because children vary so enormously in shape, weight, size, strength and agility, regardless of their age. Children who are lightweight, lithe and fit with a natural gymnastic ability can safely manage handstands against the wall, followed by shoulderstands and eventually headstands. They find them the most satisfying challenges of all and can't wait to practise them even if they are several years younger than 12, in which case it is sad to deny them. The vital element will always be starting to build up, well in advance, towards the achievement of a headstand. Toddlers and small children can be held upside down by the waist or their ankles for a few moments. Many parents already do this just for family fun.

Ensuring the child's safety will depend upon adult discretion and a building up, one 'strand at a time' over a period of time, of a child's strength and agility.

Upside down for a moment

MAKE IT FUN!

Yoga makes me able to laugh!

12 year old

These ideas may help engage younger children's interest.

Animal finger puppets (for young children/toddlers)
Invite each child to choose an animal finger puppet. Talk about it and the noise it makes and then mimic the animal together. Beanies or a favourite, floppy, soft toy work in just the same way. You may then want to practise the posture named for that animal.

Books (for toddlers up to eight year olds)
Rhyming and movement books are useful to read with children during yoga (see pages 163–166 for suggestions). Choose rhymes that involve animals which can be mimicked – for example:

> *I'm a jolly frog*
> *The happiest one alive*
> *But when the sun's too hot*
> *Into the pond I dive*

Your child will quickly learn the words and enjoy mimicking the animal even more.

You may wish to choose a book which has real heart in it for you, that has a meaning or message that resonates for you and your child. Read it aloud, ideally with your child on your lap or tucked up close beside you. Then read it again and pick out the moments when you can illustrate the story with a yoga posture. Whenever you come across an animal, bird, insect or any living creature jump up and use the yoga posture which fits – or invent one.

These books might help start you off:

For toddlers: *Mr Gumpy's Outing* by John Burningham, *Whose Eyes are These?* by Elizabeth Burman, *The Gingerbread Man* retold by Hugh Lupton

For older children: *There is a Billy Goat in the Garden* by Laurel Dee Gugler, *I Took the Moon for a Walk* by Carolyn Curtis, *The Mountains of Tibet* by Mordicai Gerstein, *Do Animals Have Feelings Too?* by David L. Rice, *The Big Big Sea* by Martin Waddell, *In the Company of Bears* by A.B. Curtiss. See resources section for further details of these books.

Flying!

Make your own Story

Here are two ideas for you to try: these stories require a trained yoga teacher to help children with the named postures. More informally, encourage children to invent their own postures to illustrate the stories.

The Cat in the Wood

There was once a big ginger cat fast asleep in the dry leaves, under a tree in the woods (*Relaxation Pose* see page 112). He was dreaming of the night sky. In his mind the stars appeared one by one until they began to make patterns and pictures in the silence of the night. He could even see the shapes of some of his animal friends shining above him.

As the dawn light began to creep into the sky, it was time to wake up. Cat stretched then curled up into a little ball (*'Ha' Breath* see page 129). He turned his head from side to side, sniffing the air and circled his paws to be ready for anything. Then he got up to stretch his spine (*Cat, Tiger, Cat Balance* see pages 96–97). Soon he began prowling through the trees, wondering what he might catch for breakfast and thinking about his dream. The Sun was beginning to warm his fur and his tummy was rumbling. Suddenly he stopped. Did he hear a strange sound? Yes! Something was snuffling and sniffling in the bushes. Cat stood up on his back paws for a moment. He could see the wagging tail of a dog with its nose down a rabbit hole (*Dog Pose* see page 102). Feeling nervous, Cat quickly climbed up the tallest tree he could find in the wood (*Swaying Palm Tree* pose followed by the *Tree* pose see pages 76 and 80). While Cat was up in the tree he could see exactly what the dog was doing. He could also see a little stream with a hare in the long grass on the far side of the water.

Cat decided to wash himself until he had calmed down. While he was licking his fur a bright butterfly appeared and flew round and round his head before softly landing on the branch beside him. *How beautiful it is* he thought, *I am going to have a try at pretending to be a butterfly* (*The Butterfly* pose see page 101). He felt quite sad when the butterfly flew off and disappeared between the tree trunks.

The dog was out of sight so it was safe for Cat to come down from the tree. He scrambled down the trunk backwards, holding onto the bark and making scraping noises with his claws. As he jumped the last few metres and landed on the grass he noticed a little movement. His whiskers twitched as he crept forward towards the stream. There on the bank beside the water was a baby hare, hopping about and panting anxiously. The mother hare, with her long legs had leapt across the stream to avoid the dog. She was calling out to her baby, but he could not swim and he was too small to jump.

Cat thought *I can help here! I am big and strong. I can use my claws to pull that branch down off the bank to make a bridge so the baby hare can cross safely and reach his mother* (*The Bridge* pose see page 105) The baby hare watched from one side of the stream as Cat built the bridge and the mother hare watched from the other side. The baby hare crossed the bridge safely and looked back at Cat. *His friendly eyes swept away my fear* he said to himself.

Cat was exhausted after climbing trees and dragging branches, and the heat of the midday Sun had made him quite sleepy. He sat down with the warmth of the Sun in his face and the sound of the bees buzzing. He purred and joined in with the sound (*Humming Bee Breath* see page 128). Soon he stretched out along the bank and felt his whole body soften and relax (*Relaxation Pose* see page 112). He could hear all the noises of the wood, smell the earth, the grass and the water. He could feel the gentle breeze in his fur and see again the pictures of the star animals in the sky of his dream.

Let's wake up and go

Start this story yoga in the Relaxation Pose (see page 112). '*Let's pretend we are still in bed*'. Then, '*Let's wake up and go to the zoo. We'll go there on our bikes.*' Here you can do appropriate warm-up exercises (see pages 69–73) and sing 'Going to the zoo'. Then, '*When we arrive at the zoo you can decide which animals we are going to see, or we'll choose in turn.*' Invent or do the appropriate yoga postures one by one, then bicycle home. Lie in relaxation (see page 112) and remember all you have seen.

Making Sounds

You may like to incorporate techniques that develop children's listening and concentration skills into yoga with children to further engage their interest. This will help a child who is easily distracted and finds it difficult to listen and be still.

First, always ask your child to sit or lie quietly, with eyes closed. Toddlers will just enjoy the calming, soothing and interesting sounds you make for them. Some of them may be itching to jump up and join in, in which case take it in turns to lie, eyes shut, listening.

Ask an older child, after listening to several sounds, to tell you what they think made the sounds and in which order they heard them. Then these sounds can be repeated but in a different order to encourage them to listen and remember. This exercise is very good at developing memory skills.

Sounds Good!

Use or invent instruments to produce different sounds. These could provide sound effects to use alongside various animal postures or a yoga story. Use any children's small instruments such as rain sticks, little bells and chimes – but add your own inventions!

- crush dried leaves or cornflakes in a bowl to give a crisp crunchy sound
- crumple paper and plastic bags
- tap your fingers on a hard surface; clap with fingers on palm, palms and fingers together or cupped hands; blow into your hands
- tap different surfaces with a cardboard roll from wrapping paper or a wooden spoon
- clap spoons together
- pour rice into a metal container slowly and steadily
- run a wooden spoon lightly along a radiator.

Make your own Yoga Storyboard

Using a large piece of card, help your child cut out and stick onto it pictures of animals and scenes of nature and invent a storyline together. You can use the storyboard to lead you and your child through different postures and sounds. For example, a camel and his journey across the desert to an oasis – everything he sees and meets on the way. You can always use your own memories and photographs of special days out and re-create them on a storyboard. Homemade stories are usually full of laughs and inventiveness. Most importantly they help children to listen, use their imagination and share ideas.

Older Children

Talk to older children about the origins of yoga. They may enjoy this mythical story about the first origins of yoga postures.

> Lord Shiva (one of India's ancient gods) created 8,400,000 living creatures and plants in the world by inventing 8,400,000 poses (asanas) with his body. Every time he did a different asana, another form of life came into being. This is why many of the (much fewer!) asanas we do today come from a living thing such as a tree, a fish or a dog. Other asanas represent the creative energy in human beings such as the plough, the boat, the bow and geometrical shapes.

When a child has made good effort in yoga practice, celebrate his or her success with a certificate of merit (see page 157 for a photocopiable sheet).

CHAPTER 6

Warm-ups and poses

WARM-UP GAMES

I love the postures and the games. Yoga helps a lot to wake me up and be on good form.

Maxime, aged 8

Each session should start with a warm-up to loosen the body and prepare the joints for yoga postures.

Pick and choose.

Whole Body Shake
- Pick up your right foot and shake your foot and ankle. Feel the shake going up the leg until your whole leg is shaking with your foot.
- Do the same with your left leg. Then, each arm in turn.
- Finally, with both feet on the floor, see if you can bring the shake right up through your whole body. For young children, make any silly noise or sing a song such as

Jelly on a plate

Jelly on a plate.

Wibble, wobble, wibble, wobble

Jelly on a plate!

Bean Game

Children walk around the room using a variety of steps: giant, small, skip, hop and tiptoe. The name of a bean is called out and the children get into the shape of the chosen bean:

● Frozen bean – freeze in Mountain Pose (see page 75)

● Kidney bean – lie in foetal position on floor

● Green bean – tall standing stretch, breathing in with arms raised above head

● Baked bean – lie on the floor and imagine being bathed in sunlight instead of tomato sauce!

Shaker Game

Shake a shaker while the children shake their feet, legs, arms and whole body. When the shaker stops, the children freeze in Mountain Pose (see page 75). To vary the game let each child take a turn with the shaker.

Hopping Frog

- Squat with legs far enough apart to have feet flat on the floor.
- Make hands into fists and cross the wrists, then bring the fists to rest on top of the head.
- Move the weight of your body up onto your toes and hop forwards several times.
- Croak!

Follow the Leader

- Choose a leader to perform a movement to warm up one part of the body, starting with the feet.
- Children walk around in a circle one behind the other. Everyone copies the leader.
- When the feet are warmed up the person behind the leader takes over and chooses the next movement.
- This continues until all parts of the body have been moved or until every child has had a turn.

Add music to develop movement and rhythm. Take turns to copy each other if it's just you and your child.

Whole Body Warm-up or Pavanmuktasana

This series of warm-up movements brings awareness to each joint and how it moves. It can either be used as the preparation for yoga or as a session on its own, possibly with singing or chanting or rhythmic background music.

These warm-up exercises mentally prepare children by bringing their attention into a focused state. All the movements are performed with awareness of the breath. Each movement is repeated from between three to six times, less or more depending on the child's age and ability to concentrate.

Toes away, Toes towards

- Sit with your legs stretched out, breathe in as you tip your toes towards yourself.
- Breathe out as you tip your toes away from yourself.

Variation
To do this standing, press your big toe down onto the floor and lift and spread the other four toes upwards. Now press your four toes down onto the floor and lift your big toe upwards.

Ankle Rotation

From standing, lift one foot off the ground at a time and circle each foot clockwise and then anti-clockwise several times. From sitting, separate your feet a little and circle each foot clockwise and then anti-clockwise.

Knee Bend

- Sit down and stretch both legs out in front of you. Place your hands under your right thigh.
- Breathe in, and as you breathe out, bend your knee up to your chest. As you breathe in, straighten that leg again without touching the floor and then lower it gently to the floor.
- Repeat with the other leg.

Hips

- Sit with legs stretched out and apart. As you breathe in, turn your toes out as far as possible and turn your hips out with them. Can you touch the floor with your little toe?
- Breathe out and turn your feet inwards. Now, can your big toes meet each other and touch the floor? Your hips will also turn inwards.

Shoulder Lifts and Rolls

- Breathe in, lift shoulders up, towards your ears, sigh out your breath as you drop them down again to relax tension. Do this three or four times.
- Place fingers on top of shoulders, bring elbows together in front of your chest as you breathe in.
- Then lift your elbows upwards and outwards, drawing a big circle, as you breathe out. Make these circles three or four times in each direction.

Elbows

- As you breathe in, stretch out your arms in front of you at shoulder level, palms facing the ceiling.
- Bring your fingertips to touch your shoulders as you breathe out.
- Repeat four times and feel the movement of your elbow joint.

Hand Shakes and Stars

- Sitting with your legs stretched out or cross-legged on the floor, put your hands on your lap, palms facing up.
- Breathe in and stick all of your fingers out to make a star shape.
- Breathe out as you clench your hands.
- Then hold your arms out and shake the hands with loose wrists, to get rid of any tension.

Variation

- Move your fingers to see the muscles pulling in the back of the hands.
- Shoot fingers out from the fists and throw arms forward in a 'light-flashing' movement.

Neck Stretches

- Sit in a cross-legged position facing forward, lower your chin to your chest and move your chin slowly like a pendulum from one side to the other to stretch the back of the neck.
- Now slowly lower your right ear towards your right shoulder. Come up again and lower your left ear towards your left shoulder. This stretches the side muscles of your neck.
- Straighten up again and look up the wall in front of you to the ceiling, then along the ceiling, first to the left and then to the right, to stretch the front of the neck. Relax again and take a slow deep breath.

Variation 1
Pretend your nose is a piece of chalk and draw ever larger circles with it.

Variation 2 **The Owl**
Two round eyes – circle each eye with thumb and forefinger.

Two tufty ears – hands up on head, facing forward.

Two claws for feet – hands with down-curved fingers at waist level.

Sitting on a branch watching you – turn head slowly to the left then to the right.

Flaps its wings and says 'Twit-twoo' – flap wings. Chin down on chest then head up to the sky.

POSES (ASANAS)

The Sanskrit word is given alongside the English translation.

Always try to visualize, like a picture in your head, the pose you are just about to do. This small pause will alert your brain to remind you exactly what movements you are going to make and so help you make them.

You will find one ☆, two ☆☆ or three ☆☆☆ to show which postures are easy and which are more of a challenge. SPECIAL CARE indicates that the posture needs particular care.

STANDING POSES

Standing poses invigorate and refresh by easing tension, aches and pains. They increase the strength of the legs, ankles and pelvis providing a firm base and support for the spine. Standing exercises help children develop correct movement and awareness of the right way to stand, walk and sit. Some of the postures are strenuous and this increases endurance levels, giving strength and mobility to the joints.

☆ *Mountain Pose* or *Tadasana*

This pose is used as the starting point for many other poses.

- Stand upright with feet together or hip-width apart if the child finds it hard to balance.
- Look straight ahead.
- Arms relaxed by the side of the body, with palms on thighs.
- Be aware of keeping the spine straight and shoulders down and relaxed.

Imagine someone is pulling a string through your spine and up through the top of your head.

- Breathe normally and hold the posture for as long as you wish.

Practise Mountain Pose while waiting in a queue – it helps your posture and patience!

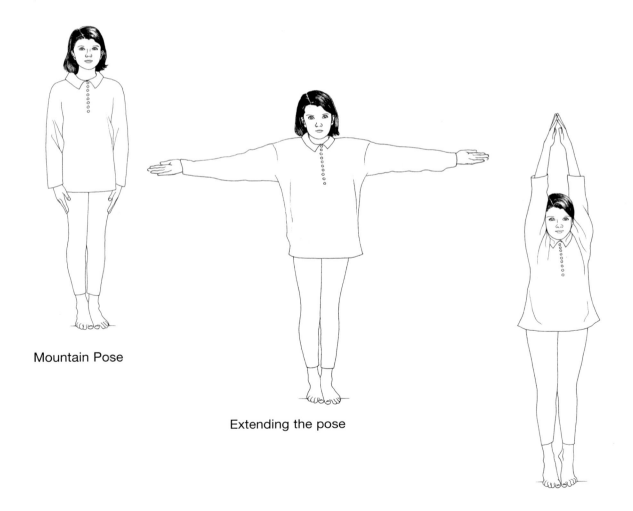

Mountain Pose

Extending the pose

Extending the pose

- In Mountain Pose, breathe out all the air you can through your nose.

- Breathe in as you rise up on your toes and lift your arms sideways until your hands touch above your head. Keep your arms straight and try to balance on your toes.

- As you breathe out again through your nose, drop your heels to the floor and bring your arms down beside you.

Visualize yourself standing on the top of a mountain or hill looking at the world spread out all around you. Feel yourself to be as strong and still as a mountain.

> 'Standing still, not running somewhere;
>
> Standing still, taking stock;
>
> Standing still, observing;
>
> Standing still, feeling and seeing.'
>
> from *Hatha Yoga: The Hidden Language* by Swami Sivananda Radha

☆ *Swaying Palm Tree* or *Tiryaka Tadasana*

- Stand in Mountain Pose (see page 75).

- Inhale as you lift your arms out in front of you and all the way up above your head, palms facing each other. Keep your hands shoulder distance apart.

- Breathe out, swaying both arms to the right and breathe in as you return to the centre. Breathe out as you sway to the left. Keep your arms by your ears at all times so your head bends with your arms.

  Imagine you are swaying in a warm breeze.

☆ *Triangle* or *Trikonasana*

In yoga, the triangle expresses harmony – the unity of mind, body and spirit.

- Stand in Mountain Pose (see page 75) and then bring your feet just wider than your hips.

- Lift your arms to shoulder level and stretch your fingers with palms down.

- Turn the left foot out till the toes are pointing the same way as your fingers. Turn the right foot in a little bit (45°); you are now triangular.

- Lift your rib cage as you breathe in. As you breathe out, bend sideways, with the left hand reaching down your left leg to a place that feels steady and comfortable without you needing to bend forward.

- Keep the legs straight with your weight firmly on the right foot. Feel your spine lengthen.

- Now, put your right hand straight up in the air. Reverse all these movements smoothly until you can step or jump back into the starting position. Repeat on the other side.

- Lean with your back against a wall to check you are not bending forward from the waist.

How many triangles can you see in this posture?

☆ *The Warrior* or *Virabhadrasana*

This posture is useful with storytelling. The peaceful, strong, brave warrior can teach children a lot about developing useful tools to help them cope when needs arise such as the ability to remain calm when there is a crisis. A true warrior is not violent or destructive as shown in some computer games. He or she is brave enough to try new things and takes good care of him or herself and others.

- Stand in Mountain Pose (see page 75), then bring your feet wide apart.
- Bring your arms up to join palms above your head. Keep your elbows strong and straight.
- Turn your right foot 90° out and turn the left foot 45° in.
- Turn your trunk to the right so it is facing the same way as the right foot. Hold steady.
- Breathe in as you stretch up as high as you can in this position
- Breathe out as you bend your right knee to make a right angle (keep your back straight). Slowly look up towards your hands.
- Reverse each movement and step back into Mountain Pose.
- Repeat with other leg.

Variation

Follow the first three steps as opposite. Then...

- Breathe in and raise your arms level with your shoulders.
- Turn your head and look along the middle finger of your right hand.
- Breathe out as you bend your right knee to make a right angle.
- Repeat with your other arm and leg.

> *At first you are stiff and when you do yoga often you loosen up and feel strong.*
>
> Nine year old

☆ The Archer or *Akarna Dhanurasana)*

This posture helps strengthen shoulders and arms – and willpower!

- Stand in Mountain Pose (see page 75).
- Take a big stride forward bending the knee of your left leg, right foot up on toes. Keep your spine upright.
- Clench your left fist and lift that arm up in front of your body straight and strong, shoulder level – as if holding the bow.
- Bend your right elbow and bring that arm up and back towards your right shoulder as if you are pulling the bow-string. Hold it and feel the strong stretch for a moment.

Visualize a target you would like to hit; send your wish, like an arrow, out into the world when you release the bow.

- Return to the original starting position and repeat on other leg.

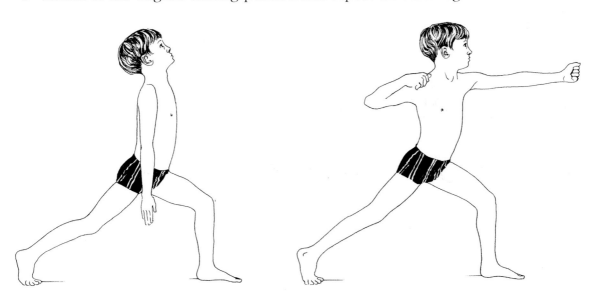

BALANCES

Balancing postures strengthen the legs, feet and ankles. They test our sense of gravity and develop our concentration.

Children love the challenge of trying to balance. In time and with practice they will be able to hold the position for longer periods, increasing their concentration and strength.

To help hold steady in a balance posture, concentrate on a spot on the wall or the floor straight in front of you. Avoid looking at other people when you are trying to balance – especially if they are wobbling!

☆ *Tree* or *Vrksasana*

Trees are our breathing partners, and are therefore essential to our lives. Throughout history trees have found their way into myths and legends and are rich in symbolism. When we practise this posture we understand and feel closer to the natural world.

- Stand in Mountain Pose (see page 75).
- Spread the toes of the left foot for balance and keep the left leg straight.
- Lift your right foot with your right hand so that the heel and sole of your foot is as high as possible against the inner thigh of your left leg.
- Steady your balance by focusing on a spot on the floor or wall and feel the whole foot (heel, ball of the foot and toes) in contact with the floor.
- Hold your arms out at shoulder level. As you breathe in, raise your arms above your head until your palms are touching.
- Repeat on the other foot.

If you need help to find your balance, put your hand against the wall or hold someone's shoulder

Visualize your favourite tree and imagine your foot rooted to the earth and your arms the branches, reaching up to the sky and growing towards the light.

As you practise this more, gradually straighten your elbows until your arms touch your ears.

Variation
Imitate your favourite tree. With your foot rooted to the floor, discover the different tree shapes you can make with your arms, fingers and other leg. You could be an old bent tree or a weeping willow. Look at the trees in your area and try to guess how old they are and which animals and insects may use them.

Like us, trees receive nourishment from above and below, from sunlight, water and earth. Oak, beech and chestnut trees can live for hundreds of years with their deep, wide-spreading and powerful roots, strong and steady trunks and long spreading branches making up the crown. These great trees may break in a storm while the willow and birch with their long slender branches can sway and bend with the force of the wind. Are you an oak or a willow when there are difficulties? There are times when we need to be flexible and bend and at other times when we need to stand firm.

☆☆ *The Eagle* or *Garudasana*

An eagle can see everything clearly – far and wide as well as nearby – reminding us to keep our eyes on the whole picture. The Eagle is a strengthening posture and helps us to balance and concentrate and to improve the circulation when the posture is released.

- Stand in Mountain Pose (see page 75).
- Lift the left foot and twist it round over the right thigh and tuck it behind the right knee. Spread the toes of your right foot to help you balance.
- Bring both hands up in front of your face. Make a twist of your arms bringing your palms together as much as you can. Keep your balance for a moment looking through the 'eye of the eagle' between your arms.
- Untwist very slowly.
- Repeat on the other leg.

Variation

Imagine you are standing on a high ledge about to take flight.

Here is a story for you called *Even Eagles Need A Push*.

The eagle gently coaxed her full-grown chicks towards the edge of the nest. Her heart quivered with conflicting emotions as she felt their resistance to her persistent nudging.

Why does the thrill of soaring have to begin with the fear of falling?

Always the same, unchanging question.

Her nest was on a ledge, high up on the sheer rock face of a cliff. Below, there was nothing but air and the pounding sea far, far beneath it.

Is it possible that this time it will not work?

Despite her fears, the eagle knew it **was** time. All her work looking after her eaglets was complete and there remained only one final task – the push. Until her chicks discovered their wings there was no purpose in their lives, no joy. The push was the greatest gift she had to offer. The eagle drew courage from her own inner wisdom. One by one she pushed them and they flew.

Adapted from *Even Eagles Need A Push* by David McNally – www.davidmcnally.com

---

☆☆ *The Dancer* or *Natarajasana*

- Stand in Mountain Pose (see page 75).
- Raise your left arm high and straight.
- Spread the toes of your left foot to help balance.
- Bend your right leg up behind you until you can hold your ankle or foot in your hand.
- Pull up your foot and reach up, stretching your whole body.

Variation

Balancing on one leg, try to make different dancing shapes. Try to find your centre of gravity.

✩✩ **Boat** or **Navasana** or **Naukasana**

SPECIAL CARE Avoid this pose if you suffer from back problems.
This posture helps you to relax.

- Lie down on your back (Relaxation Pose – see page 112).

- Breathe in slowly and deeply.

- As you breathe out again, tense your muscles and lift your head and feet so you are balancing on your bottom. Keep your legs straight and point your toes.

- Lift your arms until they are parallel to the floor and lace your fingers together strongly behind your knees, so you make a boat shape.

- Keep still as if you are in a calm harbour and breathe normally.

- Breathe out as you relax back onto the floor and breathe normally until you are steady again. Do this several times then try gently 'rocking the boat'.

If you are making up a story about a journey then the boat is a useful mode of transport. For younger children, you can sing 'Row, row, row the boat' as you do it.

TWISTS

Twists make your spine more flexible. They help release stiffness in the head and shoulders and they massage the internal organs.

✩ and ✩✩ **Spiral Spine**

Start in Stick Pose (see page 99) – sitting with your legs straight out in front.

✩ **Stage 1**

- Bend both your legs back together on the right side. Tuck your left foot under the right foot for stability.

- Turn the upper body and your head to the right, away from your knees.

- Put your right fingertips by your right hip and your left fingertips by your right knee. Stretch the spine and feel your ribs lifting. Breathe normally and stay in this position for a few seconds before continuing.

✩✩ *Stage 2*

- Turn your right hand inwards and tuck your fingers under the thigh just above the knee.

- Swing your left arm behind your back, along your waist and hold your right arm if you can. If you can't hold your right arm, just try to touch it with your fingertips.

- Twist your body further round so you can look over your right shoulder. Stay in this position for a few seconds, breathing normally.

- Release both hands, return to Stick Pose.

Repeat with legs on the left side.

✩✩ *Spinal Twist* or *Ardha Matsyendrasana*

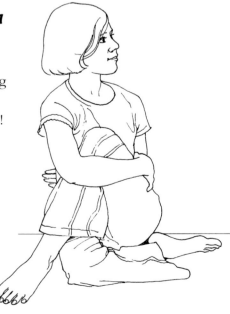

- Kneel, and sit on your heels. Place your hands on thighs, palms down.

- Move to sit to the right of your feet. Lift your left leg over your right so that your foot is on the floor up against the outside of your right knee. Back straight!

- Breathe in. Stretch your arms out to the side, shoulder level.

- Breathe out. Twist your whole upper body to the left as far as you can.

- Hug your knee towards your chest with your right arm. Move your left hand to press lightly on the floor behind you or hold your arm behind your back and lift up through the spine.

Extending the pose

- Bring your right arm down to the outside of your right knee, so that your knee is tucked behind your armpit and hold your left foot with your right hand. Put your left hand on the floor behind you.

- Breathe in. As you breathe out twist as far as possible to the left and look over your left shoulder.

- As you improve, you may be able to join your hands together behind your back. Return smoothly to the kneeling position and repeat, sitting to the left of your feet.

✩✩ *Reverse Triangle* or *Parivrtta Trikonasana*

- Start in Mountain Pose (see page 75).

- Breathe in and move feet wide apart. Stretch your arms out at shoulder level, extending your fingers, palms down.

- Turn out your right foot 90° and turn your left foot in 45°.

- Twist the whole upper body to the right, facing the same direction as the right foot.

- Keep your legs straight, lift your ribs and stretch out your arms.

- Swing your left arm down towards your ankle and creep your hand down your leg as far as you can and hold the leg or ankle.

- When you feel balanced, reach right up vertically with your right arm, elbow and fingers straight. As you hold this stretch, look at your fingers. No hip wiggling!

- Reverse the movements, jump back or step into Mountain Pose. Repeat on other leg.

☆ *Lying Twist* or *Supta Parivartanasana*

This posture is relaxing and gently twists the spine.

- Lie on your back with your knees bent up onto your chest.

- Stretch your arms out at shoulder length, resting on the floor.

- Turn the palms of your hands to face upwards. Breathe in, and as you breathe out allow your knees to fall slowly to the right. Try to keep your knees together as much as possible.

- Slowly turn your head to the left. Hold and relax into the twist, breathing evenly.

- Breathe in as you bring your head and knees back to the centre. Repeat on the other side.

Variation

Rainbow Twist

- Lie on your right side with both knees tucked into your chest, left knee on top of right knee.

- Place your right arm along the floor with your left arm on top and join the palms of your hands together.

- Breathe in, lift your left arm and draw a rainbow arc in the air all the way over to the left, turning your head to follow it until you are in the Lying Twist.

- Draw another rainbow as you bring your arm back.

- Roll over onto your left side and repeat the Rainbow Twist again.

Rainbows

The sky was dark and gloomy
When the rain had drifted by
Then suddenly like magic,
A vision filled the sky.

An arc of seven colours
All blended clear and true,
To form a perfect rainbow
In that sky of darkened blue.

These seven brilliant colours
Which compose a rainbow arc
Are signs of future promise
When the world is dull and dark.

Anonymous

FORWARD AND BACK BENDS

Forward and back bends give energy and courage. They free tightness in your chest and make your spine flexible. Your arms and shoulders become strong and your mind and body alert.

It is important to follow a back bend with a counter pose, relaxing and releasing the stretch of the back. Balance each back bend with a forward bend, unless another pose is specified.

Take special care when moving into a backwards bend. Never rush, and stop if it feels uncomfortable.

☆☆ *The Camel* or *Ushtrasana*

SPECIAL CARE Avoid this posture if you feel strain in the knees. Move slowly and carefully to avoid placing strain on your neck.

The camel may look clumsy but has adapted to life in very difficult conditions. Quite apart from carrying his own food and water supply with him in his humps, his feet help him travel for miles and get his big body up and down steep slopes, even in deep, soft sand.

- Sit on your knees (knees and feet hip distance apart) with your arms by the sides of your body.

- Keep your legs and hips strong as you breathe in and lengthen the spine. Gently lean backwards and reach for your heels.

This may be enough for some children.

- If and when you are comfortable, push your chest and tummy up and out, and then your bottom, giving your body as much of a curve as you can. Keep your legs strong and your pelvis pushing forward.

- Take your head back slowly as far as it is comfortable – but don't drop it back or use jerky movements.

- To come out of this position, slowly bring your chin onto your chest and gently move back to your original position.

- To counteract the backwards bend, bend forward until your forehead touches the floor, arms relaxed by your sides. Breathe deeply and enjoy!

☆ *Locust* or *Salabhasana*
This posture strengthens the back and energizes the body.

- Lie face down with your forehead resting on the floor, legs together, toes pointed with your arms alongside your body and the backs of your hands resting on the floor.

- Alternatively make fists and place them together, thumbs touching under your thighs.

- Breathe in deeply and press your fists against the floor to push your legs upwards as high as you can. Keep your head down and knees straight.

- Hold the pose for as long as it is comfortable.
- Breathe out and lower your legs gently.

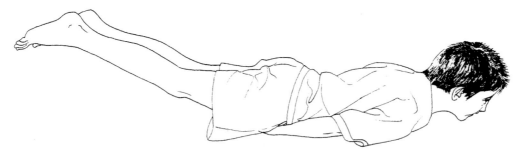

Variation

Alternate Stretch

Lie down as for Locust.

- Reach out in front of you with your arms, palms facing down. Breathe in, raise your head and chest.
- Now lift and stretch your right arm and left leg away from your centre.

Repeat on the other side.

☆ Cobra (Snake) or *Bhujangasana*

A cobra is a beautiful snake which rears up when it is about to strike. This asana helps your spine to bend well.

- Lie face down, legs together, toes pointed, palms of hands on the floor beneath your shoulders, fingers forward.
- As you breathe in, push on your hands until your arms are straight, so your upper body lifts.
- Keep your hips on the floor and arch your back as much as possible and is comfortable. Look up towards the ceiling or straight ahead, puffing your chest out like a cobra ready to strike.
- After a few seconds, bend your elbows as you breathe out and lower yourself onto the floor. Relax.

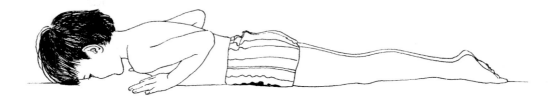

*'Snake, snake sleepy snake, sleepy snake won't hiss.
Snake, snake wide awake hisses just like this.'*

You or the children can chant this, and hiss the breath out, coming out of the posture.

☆☆☆ *Swan* or *Hamsasana*

Swan is really the full cobra posture but it is much more like a swan resting
on the surface of a lake. A graceful swan, swimming slowly on a
river, ready to dive for weed, is a beautiful sight. This asana
will make your spine so supple that you will become as
graceful as a swan.

- Follow the first step for Cobra Pose (see page 89).
- As you breathe in, push on your hands and raise your body (higher than in Cobra)
  and arch your spine so that only your legs and your hands are on the floor.
- Breathe normally and bend your
  knees so that your feet come up
  and point towards your head.
- How far can your toes
  comfortably move towards
  the back of your head?
- Return slowly to the lying
  down position and relax.

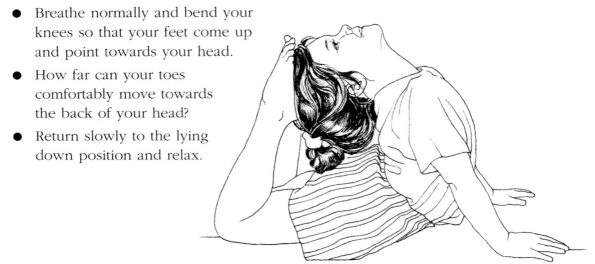

✮✮ *The Bow* or ***Dhanurasana***

You have been an archer (see page 79) and now you are going to be the bow and make yourself as supple as bendy wood!

- Lie face down on the floor with arms by your sides.

- Bring one foot up in the air and clasp it with your hand and then do the same with the other foot. Get a firm grip on the ankles if you can – or if that is hard, hold your feet.

- Breathe in, and raise your head, chest and knees off the floor as you hold onto your feet. Look up to feel the stretch in your thighs.

- Breathe normally and hold the pose for a few seconds to feel the stretch in your spine.

- Lower your body and relax.

✮ *Spinal Roll* or ***Jhulana Lurhakanasana***

This asana will fill you with energy and massage the whole of your spine.

- Place a blanket on one half of the mat for this movement. Sit at the other end of the mat so that when you roll backwards your spine will be cushioned.

- Lie flat on your back. Fold your legs onto your chest and place your hands under your thighs. Now swing up into a sitting position with your feet on the floor.

- Keeping your chin tucked into your chest, your head forwards and your spine rounded, roll backwards. Bring your feet as far back over your head as you can.

- Roll forwards and back again, finding your own rhythm. As you gather momentum, you will be able to get your feet further and further behind you. Eventually you will be able to touch the floor behind your head with your toes.

Variation
Knees on Chest

- Relax on the floor, bending both knees up onto your chest.
- Every time you breathe out gently squeeze your knees in towards you.
- Relax again as you breathe in.

This movement can be used as a counter pose for back bends.

Use the Spinal Roll instead of Shoulderstand for young children until they are at the stage in their development when they have abdominal strength and have reached full spinal development – usually around the age of 12. See also page 104 for Legs Against the Wall, another alternative for Shoulderstand.

☆☆ Floating Fish or Matsyasana

SPECIAL CARE

Ensure the weight of the body is on the elbows and NOT on the top of the head when the head is tilted back. Stop immediately and come out of this posture if there is any discomfort at this point for an individual child.

- Lie flat on the floor on your back, arms at your sides, palms under your bottom or close to your bottom, like a fish lying in a cool mountain stream. Close your eyes.
- Breathe in and raise your chest off the floor, using your elbows as a support.
- Tilt your head back gently until the top of your head is resting on the floor.
  This creates a bridge between the top of the head and the lower back.
- Breathe normally while you hold the pose and then slowly lower your head and back to return to the first position and relax. Now pull your knees up onto your chest. Follow this with the Child Pose (see page 100).

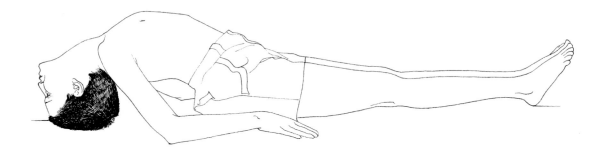

Variation

- You can do a relaxing version of this posture by rolling a blanket up like a sausage so it is the length of your spine to your head, and the same width as your body.

- Lie on the blanket and let your shoulders and arms relax down on either side of the blanket. This position will relax your chest and help the flow of breath.

☆☆ *The Wheel* or *Chakrasana*

A large gym ball can be a useful prop for this posture. Lie backwards onto it for a moment to stretch your back muscles and to prepare them for the effort needed for this posture.

- Lie in Relaxation Pose (see page 112) – flat on your back, arms to sides.

- Bend your knees up until your heels touch your bottom, feet about 30cm apart.

- Lift your arms, with bent elbows, up over your head and place the palms of your hands on the floor just above your shoulders. Check your fingers are pointing towards your shoulders.

- As you breathe in, slowly lift your hips away from the floor up into the air. As you continue lifting your chest, you will discover that the top of your head is resting lightly on the floor.

- Now straighten your arms and legs, lift your head off the floor and raise your body until it is arching like a bow.

- To come out of this pose, lift your head to look up at the ceiling, bend your knees and elbows, and gently lower your back flat onto the floor.

- Breathe out as you bring your knees up onto your chest. Then stretch out to lie flat and relax for a few breaths.

☆ *Folded Leaf* or **Uttanasana**

This posture gives a stretch to the whole back of your body.

- Stand in Mountain Pose (see page 75).

- As you breathe out, slowly fold forwards and down with your knees bent.

- As you bend forwards, clasp your hands together behind your thighs and slide your hands gently down, trying to straighten your legs – but bend your legs if you need to. Only bend as far as comfortable.

- Let your body's weight help you relax the upper body downwards as you bring your chest closer towards your thighs. Finally relax the head.

- If your back feels uncomfortable, keep your knees bent.

- Hold this pose for a moment and then gently return to the upright position.

Imagine you are an open book about to close.

Variation
Rag Doll

Repeat the same posture with bent knees. This is a relaxing counter pose for some of the more strenuous standing postures.

☆ *Knee-to-head Stretch* or **Janusirsasana**

This posture massages the stomach and stretches the lower back.

- Sit in Stick Pose (see page 99) with legs straight out in front.

- Without moving your right leg, bend your left knee sideways and backwards, and press the heel up into the top of your right thigh. Breathe in, and as you breathe out bend at the hips, lower your body and stretch your arms forwards until you can hold your right ankle or shin in both hands. As you become more supple, try to lace your fingers under your foot.

- Then breathe in and look up. Keep your shoulders back.

- Now, as you breathe out, drop your head and take your body forwards over your right leg. Try to touch your knee with your nose if you can! Breathe normally for a few moments.

- Breathe in as you come up and straighten your back into Stick Pose.
- Repeat with other leg.

I like the stretchy poses – they make me feel light and free.

12 year old

☆ *Sandwich Pose* or *Paschimottanasana*

- Sit in Stick Pose (see page 99) with legs straight out in front in a right angle. Keep your head and back straight. Don't ever force yourself!
- Breathe in, stretching upwards. As you breathe out, hinging at the hips, bring your chest down towards your thighs with hands stretched out towards your feet.

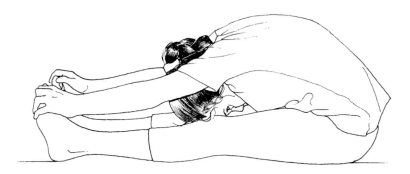

This posture is called Sandwich Pose because the legs become one slice of bread, the torso the other slice. Your hands spread the filling on the legs and you make the sandwich by bringing your torso down onto your thighs.

KNEELING AND SITTING POSES

Kneeling and sitting poses help calm the nerves and help you sleep. They increase the flexibility of your legs, ankles and hips.

☆ *The Cat* or *Marjarasana*

Next time you see a cat waking up, watch its movements! Their spines are very flexible.
A series of movements:

- Get on your hands and knees in a crawling position.
- Place your hands under your shoulders, knees under your hips. Tuck your bottom underneath you.
- Breathe out and arch your back upwards and lower your head between your arms.
- Breathe in and dip your back downwards in a curve and look up towards the ceiling.

Variation 1
The Cat Balance

- Follow the first two steps of Cat Pose.
- Lift and stretch your right arm in front of you, parallel with the floor.
- Lift and stretch your left leg straight out behind you, parallel with the floor.
- Balance for a moment or two, before repeating the balance with the opposite arm and leg.

Variation 2
The Tiger or **Vyaghrasana**

- Follow the first two steps of Cat Pose.

  - As you breathe in, raise your right leg as high as you can behind you, pointing your toes. Lift your chin up as high as you can.

    - As you breathe out slowly, bring your right knee down under your body towards your chest. Tuck your head in so your forehead tries to touch your knee.

      - Return to Cat Pose and repeat using the left leg.

☆☆ The Hero or **Virasana**

SPECIAL CARE Take care not to place strain on the knees.

Who would your hero be and why? It doesn't have to be someone famous, it can be anyone you know and admire.

- Kneel, sitting on your heels, hands by your sides, spine straight. Keep your head and neck in line.

- Carefully move your feet outwards until they are alongside and touching your hips, so you are sitting between your feet. If it feels comfortable, try to keep your knees together.

- Put the palms of your hands on your knees.

- Shoulders relaxed, lift your ribs to get a straight back. Look straight ahead with relaxed eyes. Hold this pose as long as you can.

This may be used as a meditation pose, or as a posture for doing breathing exercises. If your knees hurt in this position place a foam block or big book underneath your bottom to relieve the strain. Do not place strain on your knees.

☆ *The Hare* or *Shashankasana*

This posture has a very calming effect and is a useful counter pose to use after back bends to relax the muscles along the spine.

- Kneel, sit on heels, palms on thighs, fingers forwards. Close your eyes.

- Hold one wrist with the other hand behind your back, like the hare's ears folded along its back.

- Breathe in fully, then breathe out as you bend forwards until your chest rests on your thighs and your forehead rests on the floor in front of your knees, like the hare hiding in its 'form'.

- Hold the pose for a moment and, as you breathe in, slowly return to the upright position.

☆ *The Prayer Pose* or *Vajra-shashankasana*

This posture helps breath and movement co-ordination and creates a sense of peace.

- Kneel and sit on your heels.

- Place your hands on your knees, fingers forward, palms down. Close your eyes and be very still and relaxed. Be aware of your whole body.

- Breathe in slowly as you raise your arms above your head, palms together.

  - Breathe out slowly as you bend forwards from the waist, until your chest rests on your thighs and your forehead touches the floor in front of your knees.

  - Stretch your arms out in front of your body but turn your hands until the palms rest on the floor.

  - Breathe normally while you hold the posture for 10 seconds.

  - Breathing in, return slowly to the upright position, and repeat.

Try to breathe slowly, co-ordinating your breath with the movements.

☆ *The Lion* or *Simhasana*

Imagine you are fierce and hungry and full of pride, like the 'king of beasts'!

- Kneel and sit on your heels, feet together.

- Place the palms of your hands on your thighs, fingers forward.

- Relax your face and breathe calmly.

- Suddenly open your eyes very wide and GLARE! At the same time stick your tongue out and try to touch your chin with it. Shoot out your arms low in front of you with fingers stretched wide, as fast and as strongly as you can. ROAR!

- Hold this pose for a few seconds and then relax slowly. Can you notice how calm you feel?

This posture is good for clearing the throat and warding off colds if practised at the first signs. It helps to release anger with the outburst of breath as you roar.

I love the lion pose – it makes me happy and I love its surprising pose.

Ten year old

☆ *Stick Pose* or *Dandasana*

This pose is the basis for sitting poses and twists.

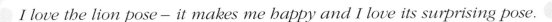

- Sit on the floor with legs stretched out in front, feet together.

- Place your palms on the floor beside your hips, fingers pointing forwards.

- Stretch your legs and heels forward (don't point your toes!). Press the backs of your knees and thighs down onto the floor.

- As you press down on your hands, stretch the sides and back, by lifting the ribs. Keep your shoulders back and down, your chest open.

- Breathe steadily and look straight ahead. Do not let your head dip down!

☆ *Child Pose* or *Pindasana*

This pose is a favourite with children. In stories, the pose can become a mouse, a hedgehog or any other small creature. It has a very calming effect and is a useful counter pose after back bends to relax the muscles along the spine.

- Kneel, sit on your heels, hands on knees, fingers forward. Close your eyes.
- As you breathe in, let your arms hang down by your sides.
- As you breathe out, lower your chest to your thighs and your forehead to the floor in front of your knees.
- As you do this, let your hands slide backwards palms up, along the floor beside your body.
- Arms lie loose and limp. Breathe normally as you hold this pose. Enjoy!

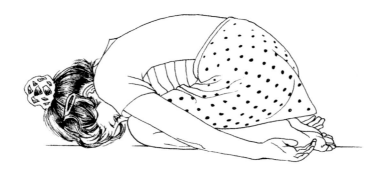

☆ *Easy Cross-legged Pose* or *Sukhasana*

- Sit cross-legged with both ankles touching the floor.
- Put your hands on your knees, palms down.
- Keep your back and neck straight, lifting up the spine from the pelvis. Make sure your shoulders are down and relaxed. Feel your chest open and breathe normally.

☆ *The Butterfly* or ***Baddha Konasana***

This pose will help you prepare for the Lotus postures.

- Sit with your spine straight. Hold your toes and bring the soles of your feet together, heels close to your body.

- Put your hands on your knees and gently apply pressure to either both knees or one at a time while breathing slowly and steadily. Keep a straight back.

- Now clasp your feet again and gently move your knees up and down (without your hands to push them). Imagine your legs are moving like a butterfly's wings for the first time, slowly opening and closing.

☆☆ *Half Lotus* or ***Ardha Padma-asana***

SPECIAL CARE Lotus posture needs working up to slowly and carefully to avoid straining ligaments in the knees and the hip joint. Practise the Easy Cross-legged Pose and the Butterfly first.

Padma means Lotus. The lotus flower has been a symbol of beauty in many parts of the world for thousands of years. People discovered long ago that if they 'locked' their legs while sitting down, they could be comfortable for a long time and not fall over. Even if you fall asleep, you cannot topple over! This is why the pose is often used for meditation.

- Sit with your right leg stretched in front of you and bend the other leg until the sole of your foot lies against the thigh, so the heel is as close to your body as it will go.

- Bend your left knee and with both hands, lift your left foot up into the air, pointing towards your forehead and place it, sole up on top of your upper right thigh. If there is any pull in the knees, return to practising the Butterfly (see above) until your flexibility increases.

- Now put your hands on your knees, palms down. Press down gently to straighten your spine. Be very careful how you do it, and if you find it hard, just practise day-by-day until it gets easier as your muscles stretch.

- Repeat, changing feet positions.

> *The lotus is a symbol of purity. Lotus seeds sprout in the dark, murky bottom of ponds. The stems grow upwards searching for the light, and on the surface of the water the beautiful flowers bloom creamy-white and pink.*

☆☆☆ *Full Lotus* or *Padma-asana*

SPECIAL CARE Avoid straining your knees.

Only practise this posture when you have mastered the Half Lotus.

The Full Lotus is the same as the Half Lotus but the foot which rests on the floor is also lifted up and rests, sole up, on the opposite thigh.

INVERTED POSES

Inverted Poses revitalize the whole system. They stimulate the inner organs and therefore improve the circulation and tone the glands. They improve the concentration by increasing blood flow to the brain. They can help sound sleep.

☆ *Dog Pose* or *Svanasana*

A dog is a man's best friend and a loyal companion when cared for properly and given plenty of exercise. A dog's sense of smell is far beyond ours. Share your experiences of different kinds of dogs and their special qualities before you do this posture.

- Lie face down on the floor, with your feet the same width apart as your hips and your hands on the floor under your shoulders. Fingers must be spread to help your balance.

- Tuck your toes up under your heels and come up into the crawling position on your knees, with straight arms. Check your arms and feet are in line.

- Straighten your legs and push your bottom high into the air to make a triangle shape.

- Tuck your chin down to your chest so that your head is relaxed between your arms, and extra blood can reach your brain.

The more you practise, try to get your heels on the floor – it's quite a challenge!

Variation for two!
One can be in the Dog Pose and another can do the Cobra Pose (see page 89) underneath. The dog can become a bridge or a mountain.

> Young children's necks are still slender and delicate, so the following postures should be done with special care. Please reread the guidelines concerning Shoulderstand and Plough on page 63.

☆☆☆ *Plough* or *Halasana*
SPECIAL CARE Do not put any pressure on your neck.

- Lie flat on your back with your arms at your sides.
- Raise both your legs, keeping them straight until they are vertical.
- Press down with your hands and lift your legs and body up so that your legs can move over your head towards your nose. As you swing your legs back over your head, your bottom will come up off the ground. Now lower your legs as far as you can. Support your back with your hands if need be.
- Keeping the legs straight if you can, try to get your toes on the floor way behind your head. Breathe normally for a moment. You may find it hard to do this with straight legs, in which case keep the knees bent. The head must be kept still all the time.
- To come out of the posture, keep your head on the floor and bend your knees in towards your forehead. Keep them bent as you slowly lower your spine onto the floor again then slide your legs down until they are flat on the floor. Relax on your back.

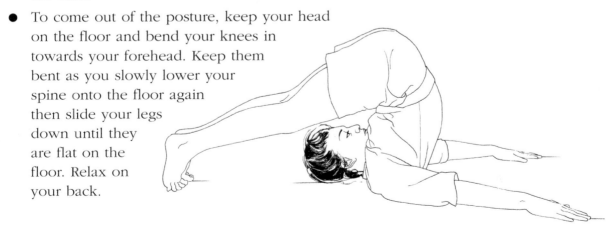

Variation
For a more challenging variation, follow the first three steps and then reach back with one leg and leaving the other leg vertical. Then swap legs.

☆☆☆ *Shoulderstand* or *Candle Pose* or *Sarvangasana*

SPECIAL CARE Ensure your weight is on your shoulders, not your neck. If you feel any pressure in your face, come out of the pose.

- Lie down flat on your back, with your arms down at your sides.

- Raise your legs with knees bent and then straighten them out and bring them back over and above your head so that your bottom comes off the ground.

- Give yourself a little further push upwards, bend your elbows and slip your hands into the small of your back to support yourself, fingers behind and thumbs in front.

- First make sure that your legs are really straight and then try to move them into the vertical position like candles on a birthday cake. Keep your shoulders on the ground to take your weight so that your legs can stay upright and balance easily. Your legs should be straight and your chin pressing your chest.

  DO NOT MOVE YOUR HEAD FROM SIDE TO SIDE. THE WEIGHT SHOULD BE ON THE SHOULDERS, NOT THE HEAD.

- When you feel you have stayed there long enough, slowly bend your knees and bring them down towards your nose. Lower your arms onto the floor, pressing down to help support the weight of your lower body as you slowly uncurl. Lie on your back in Relaxation Pose and enjoy the feeling!

The Lying Twist (see page 86) and the Floating Fish (see page 92) are the counter poses for Shoulderstand.

☆ *Legs Against the Wall*

Like the Spinal Roll this can help children prepare for an eventual Shoulderstand.

- Sit with your left side alongside the wall. Lie down with knees bent over your chest.

- Move your top half round and bring your legs to lie flat and straight up against the wall so that you are making a right angle with the wall and the floor. Make sure your head, neck and spine are in alignment.
- If this feels comfortable, slowly walk your feet upwards as high as you can, lifting your hips and spine away from the floor using the wall to support you. Use your hands to support your back.

☆ *The Bridge* or *Setu Bandha*

- Lie down flat on your back with your arms at your sides.
- Bend your knees to bring your heels as close to your bottom as possible.
- Arch the back and lift your stomach up while bringing the hips off the floor.
- Bend the elbows and place your hands on your waist, thumbs towards your stomach, fingers towards your spine.
- Hold this position as long as you are comfortable. Breathe smoothly and evenly.

Variation

If a child is adept and comfortable in Bridge, he or she can extend the posture.

- Begin to slide your feet away from the body with the soles of the feet flat on the floor.
- Breathe normally and hold this position as long as you feel comfortable.
- Lower your bottom to the floor and relax.

FLOWING POSE MOVEMENTS

These movements are especially exhilarating and enjoyable. They develop speed, concentration and stamina.

☆☆ *Greetings to the Sun* or *Surya Namaskar*

This is a whole yoga lesson and tonic in itself! Every muscle, joint and all major internal organs are stretched, moved and massaged. Namaskar means Greetings.

1 ● Face the Sun – or each other in a circle! Stand upright with feet together and palms together touching your chest.

   ● Check that your spine is straight but not rigid, and that your whole body, including your arms, is completely relaxed. Breathe normally for a moment. Call out "Namaskar".

2 ● Breathe in deeply as you raise your outstretched arms above and behind you.

   ● Tilt your pelvis forward as you arch your back. Look up at your hands.

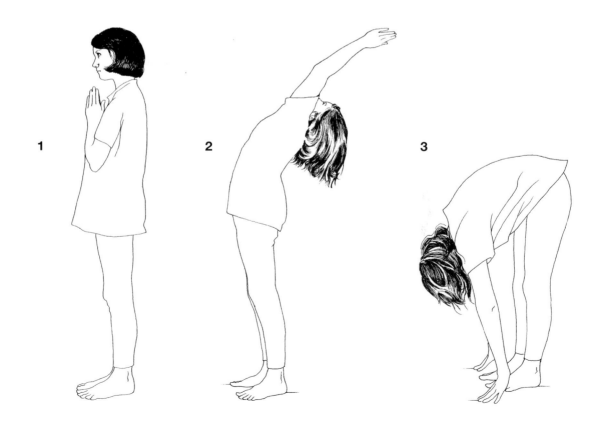

3 ● Breathe out fully as you bend forwards slowly at the hips.

● Bring your head and trunk as close to your legs and your fingertips as close to your feet as possible. Keep your legs straight, but bend your knees if you need to.

4 ● Breathe in deeply as you bend your right knee and slowly move your left leg back, stretched out behind as far as you can reach. Your left toes and knee should touch the floor and your hands should be on the floor at shoulder width on either side of your right foot.

● Arch your back and look up.

5 ● Breathe out fully as you slowly move your right leg back – so your feet are together again.

● Push your bottom high in the air to make a triangle, with your chin tucked into your chest and your head down between your arms, in Dog Pose (see page 102).

6 ● Breathe in deeply as you lower your knees slowly to the floor and bring your chest between your hands until your toes, knees, chest, hands and chin are all resting on the floor, elbows bent up like wings. Breathe normally in this position for a moment. Practise lowering yourself so smoothly that your knees, chest and chin touch down at the same time.

7 ● Breathe in deeply as you push your thighs down onto the floor, lifting your chin and shoulders at the same time, and arching your body back, elbows straight (in Cobra Pose, see page 89).

● Look straight ahead and breathe out slowly.

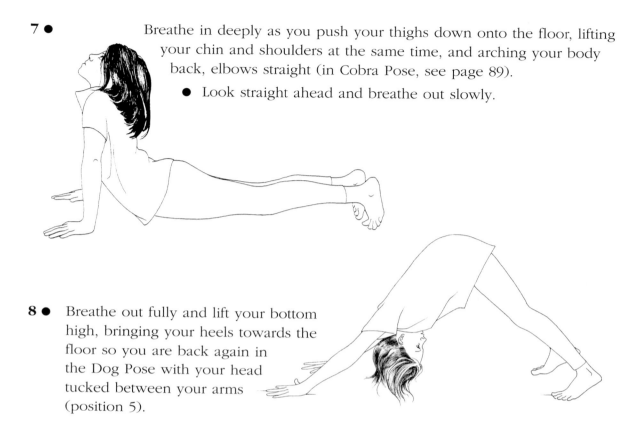

8 ● Breathe out fully and lift your bottom high, bringing your heels towards the floor so you are back again in the Dog Pose with your head tucked between your arms (position 5).

9 ● Now you are working backwards again through each position.

● Return to position 4 – breathe in, bringing your right foot forwards between your hands, your left foot reaching back, head up.

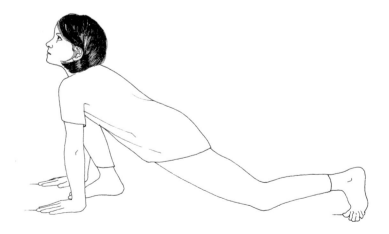

10 ● Return to position 3 – breathe out, bringing your left foot forwards to join the right foot.

● Bend at the hips to bring your forehead towards your knees, with your bottom high.

11 ● Return to position 2, breathing in and raise your body upright, outstretched arms right up over your head, pelvis tilted forwards, back arched.

12 ● Return to position 1, breathing out and coming gently back to the Namaskar greetings position, palms together on chest, standing straight and relaxed – and let your breathing return to normal.

Repeat the 12 stages, but bending your left knee and putting your right leg back in position 4 and, of course, reversing the feet positions in position 9 too.

☆☆ *Greetings to the Moon*

Greetings to the Moon is very similar. Here it is presented in pictures.

RELAXATION POSES

The relaxation is lovely. It stretches you out and it's fun. Afterwards we do drawing.

12 year old

☆ *Relaxation Pose* or *Savasana*

Always finish a yoga session with this asana. It can also help children to get to sleep quickly and peacefully when they go to bed. You may wish to place a blanket over each child for warmth and a bean bag over their eyes to help relaxation.

- Lie flat on your back with your knees bent up and your arms crossed over your chest as if you are hugging yourself, to make sure your back is really flat against the floor. Younger children and toddlers may want to hold a favourite soft toy. Gently close your eyes and mouth. Lie like this for a moment.

- Now breathe out, stretch your legs out straight and let your arms flop down at your sides, palms up. Your feet should be apart, falling outwards in a V shape if that is comfortable. Let your whole body feel limp and relaxed, like a rag doll. Don't move any part of your body. Feel your breath flowing in a natural and easy rhythm. Concentrate just on your breath as it flows in and out. You will notice that your breathing will begin to slow down and you will feel calm and peaceful.

- Guide the children to concentrate on each part of their body, making sure that each muscle is free of tension. You could say, for example "clench your toes … and relax them; press your knees down … and relax them; ball your fists … and relax them; screw up your eyes and mouth … and relax them." Work through from the tips of your toes to the top of your head.

It is important to end the relaxation exercise slowly and carefully, to gain maximum benefit.

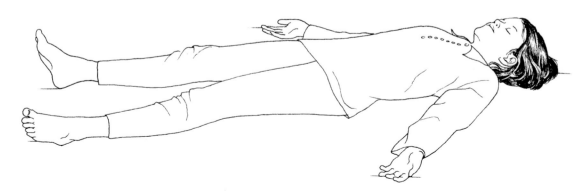

- So (if you are not in bed going peacefully to sleep!), bring your mind back to where you are and the things and the people around you. Stretch your whole body as you lie there and let your breathing return to normal.

- When you feel ready, slowly roll over onto your right side (the side away from the beating of your heart) and bend your right knee up to support you in a comfortable position – both knees if you prefer. Rest like this for as long as you want, then slowly sit up into an easy cross-legged position.

- Feel and enjoy the peace that is still with you.

YOGA PATTERNS

To make something whole and beautiful out of a group of children moving in unison is fun and creates a sense of capability and togetherness.

There are many asanas which, when done in a circle or double circle, have a wonderful overall effect. Encourage the children to play around with ideas and to experiment. Here is one example:

☆☆ *The Blossoming Lotus Flower*
SPECIAL CARE Take care when moving from lying to sitting. Roll onto your side if you have a weak back. Do not raise your legs if you have a weak back.

If there are enough of you and enough space, make either one or two circles, facing inwards towards each other with your feet in the middle of the circle. There are many variations of this. Adapt it to suit your needs.

- Lie flat on your back, arms on the floor above your head, heels together. Breathe in slowly.

- Come to sitting position. Breathe out and raise your arms up.

- Bend forwards towards the toes, reaching towards the centre of the circle.

- In a single movement, as you breathe in, return to the lying position but with your arms by your sides (you may need to roll from sitting to lying). Raise your left leg above your head, then the right leg to join it.

If you feel comfortable, extend both legs further until your hips lift off the floor and you can support them with your hands, thumbs forwards, fingers behind. Bring your legs vertical. If appropriate, older children can then lift up into the Shoulderstand for two seconds, then swing them into Plough Pose, see page 103.

- Carefully, lower your legs and come back to sitting position with your arms stretched up.
- Bend forward towards the toes, reaching towards the centre of the circle.
- Each time try to keep in rhythm with the person on either side of you.

Any children unable to join in can be the stamen of the Lotus Flower and stand at the centre of the circle slowly raising their arms as the 'petals' open outwards around them.

PARTNER POSES

☆ *The Friendship Tree*

- Stand side by side, arms down, not quite touching each other.

- Both partners bend their outside legs at the knees and place the soles of their outside feet on the inside of their thighs, just above the knees. You can use your hands to lift the foot into its right position.

- Each child stretches the inside arm upwards above the head joining the palm with the partner's palm.

- Then bring the outside arm to the middle and partners join palms together. Help each other to balance by holding very still.

☆☆☆ *Fish under Bridge*

- One partner positions herself in The Wheel pose (see page 93).

- The second partner lies in the Fish pose (see page 92), extending it with Butterfly or Lotus, and holding her hands like a fin beneath the 'bridge'. She holds the posture briefly, then comes out of the pose and 'swims' through the bridge to allow the partner to come out of The Wheel safely.

☆☆ *Sailing Boat*

- Begin with partners sitting face to face on the floor with each partner's legs bent at the knees, the soles of their feet on the floor and their toes touching. The exact distance between them will be determined by the length of their arms.

- Clasping hands at the wrists, partners match the soles of their feet together and raise and extend their legs upwards until straight.

☆ The Comet

- Start by sitting side by side, hips touching and facing forward.

- Stretch your legs out in front.

- Bend the knee of the outside leg, bringing the sole of the foot to rest somewhere comfortable on the inside edge of the thigh.

- Twist and turn to face each other. Lift and stretch your arms out at shoulder height and join hands with your partner.

☆ Crossgate

- Kneel side by side, about a metre apart, facing forward (the right distance will be determined by leg length and flexibility).

- Both partners extend their inside legs sideways, towards each other, crossing at the ankles or mid-leg.

- Breathe in and stretch up with the outside arms.

- As you breathe out, bend in towards the centre to take hold of your partner's hand above and slide the inside hands onto your knees.

☆ *See-saw*

- Sit facing each other, feet to feet as much as possible. This will depend on whether your legs are the same length or not.

- Partners move their legs apart as far as it is comfortable for each person and hold each other's hands.

- Sit up tall with straight backs. Swing rhythmically backwards and forwards, with one partner leaning back while the other partner stretches forwards.

☆ *Back Rest*

- Partners sit back-to-back with legs stretched out, feet together, in front of them.

- One partner moves into a forward bend, hands on ankles while the second partner bends backwards resting on the other's bent back.

- Arms can be raised up over the head in line with the spine. Now reverse the movement.

SEQUENCES

✰✰ *Flamingo Sequence*

Older children will enjoy this sequence. It challenges their ability to concentrate. Use a wall to lean against lightly if you feel wobbly to begin with. Breathe in with each upward movement, breathe out on each forward movement. Breathe normally when you are still, holding a position.

1. Stand in Mountain Pose (see page 75).

2. Gently raise your left leg and rest your left heel above the right knee.
   With the knee pointing forwards, place your right hand over the left hand on your left knee.

3. Gently bend forward from the hips and swing both arms lightly backwards.
   Hold in this position for a moment.

4. Straighten up again and sweep arms overhead.
    Stretch up from your right foot to the top of your head.

5. Bend gently forwards from the hips so your head rests lightly on your left knee.
    Fold both hands over your left foot. Hold.

6. Now reverse all the movements you have made.
    As number 4, straighten upwards and sweep your arms over your head again.
    Hold.

7. As number 3, bend forward from the hips and sweep the arms lightly backwards. Hold.

8. As number 2, lightly raise your left leg and rest your left heel above the right knee. Place right hand over the left hand on your left knee. Hold.

9. Stretch your left leg in front of you then return to Mountain Pose.

Begin all over again but this time raising the right leg.

☆☆☆ *Evening Wind Down Sequence*

This series of poses is for bedtime. It helps to take away the tensions of the day and can promote sound sleep. Follow the 16 photographs in sequence.

Do Legs Against the Wall (see page 104) as an alternative to Shoulderstand.

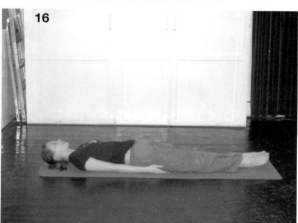

The children find it hard to balance. What can I do?
Nothing. Let them find their own centre. When balancing, it helps to focus on a point on the floor or wall.

They get the giggles and I find that frustrating.
Let them giggle. If yoga becomes a source of tension between you, leave it and come back to it later.

CHAPTER 7

Simple breathing exercises

> *Respiratory diseases are often due to "mouth breathing", whereas we should be encouraging children to breathe through their nostrils, as yoga does, because the air is warmer and filtered.*

Usha Deari, The Hale Clinic, London

The breathing exercises used in yoga are called 'pranayama'. Prana means 'life force' and yama means 'control'.

There is an intriguing fable in the *Upanishads*, a great written collection of Indian wisdom, which emphasizes the importance of the breath.

Once there was a dispute between the eyes, the ears, the speech, the mind and the breath, as to who was the most important. They all approached Lord Brahma, their spiritual leader, and asked him:

"Pray tell us, who is the greatest among us?"

"That's easy," Brahma said. "Each of you leave the body for a year. The body will then decide who among you is the greatest."

Following Brahma's advice, first the tongue went off, leaving the body without speech for a whole year. When the tongue came back the eyes went off, leaving the body blind for a year. When the eyes returned the ears went off, leaving the body deaf for a year. When the ears returned the mind went off and the body remained like a stupid simpleton for a whole year. Then the mind returned.

Next it was the turn of the breath to leave the body. As soon as the breath began to depart the tongue lost its power of speech, the eyes lost their power to see, the ears lost their ability to hear and the mind lost its intelligence! "Come back, come back, oh breaths," they prayed, "for you are the greatest among us!" The breath then returned and the body became whole again.

Some older children may enjoy this story before they begin their breathing exercises.

Breathing is something we are not taught to do because it operates at the edge of our awareness. Just as we can decide on how many times to chew on a piece of food, so we can adjust the rhythm, the tone and the timing of our breath – like a musical instrument – to suit our needs.

Feeling each other's breathing

Most children usually breathe well naturally – using the whole of their lungs. To make sure that we continue to do this, it is worth doing some breathing exercises sometimes to remind ourselves how important this is.

Until the age of eight, do only simple practices such as Blowing Feathers and Humming Bee Breath, Hissing Balloon Breath and The Complete Breath (see below). These provide a good foundation for developing controlled breathing (pranayama) later on.

Pranayama has a direct effect on the brain and emotions leaving the mind clear and the emotions steady and under our control. We feel and keep much fitter because we get more oxygen into our bloodstream and we clear out the stale air more efficiently. The nervous system is calmed and soothed.

A lot of people are 'mouth-breathers'. Whenever we are aware of our breath we should breathe in through the nose because the nose has the special purpose of warming and filtering our breath before it reaches the lungs.

Children who suffer from asthma will benefit especially from the breathing exercises, as they strengthen the breathing muscles and allow an easier outbreath. This will help them to stay calm when they have an asthma attack.

The Complete Breath

Use a small, soft toy to place on your child's tummy to practise breathing awareness when lying on the floor. She feels the toy lift when breathing in, and lower when breathing out. It can also be very comforting for a child to have a soft piece of material laid across the eyes – a light pressure helps relaxation around the eyes. This feeling will spread. Try it yourself too and see what a difference it makes.

- Lie flat on your back with your knees bent, heels against your sitting bones, hip-distance apart. Put your arms by your sides.

- Check that your spine and neck are straight. With your bent elbows on the floor, lift and spread your fingers on your tummy with your middle fingers just touching. Take a couple of breaths to relax.

- As you breathe in, slowly and deeply through your nose, feel the abdomen rise and your fingertips pull apart.

- Breathe out and feel the abdomen lower and your fingers touch again. This pushes down your diaphragm (the sheet of muscle between your chest and your abdomen).

- Now, move your hands wider apart and place them on the sides of your chest. As you breathe in, feel the air push the ribs outwards and upwards.

- Next, move your hands to just below the clavicle bones at the top of the chest and feel the slight movement there. If you breathe too deeply for too long you may begin to feel light-headed. One deep breath for each movement is enough. Focus on breathing smoothly and evenly.

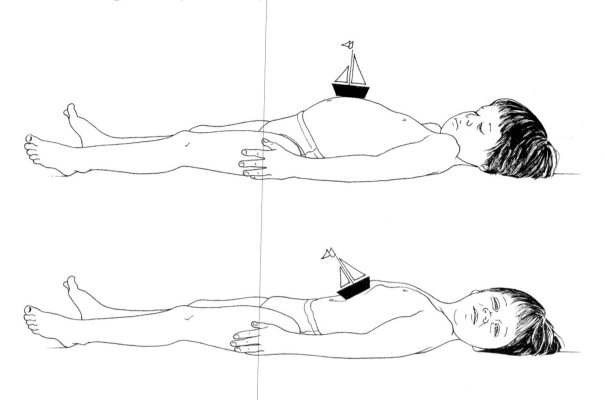

For younger children, it is especially fun to balance a small paper boat on the navel and make it rock on the big waves created by breathing in and out properly. Then move the boat higher up onto the chest and finally to the top of the chest near the neck. Notice how much the boat moves in these three places. Where is the most movement?

Humming Bee Breath or Brahmari

When a whole group does this together it sounds like a swarm of bees.

- Sit cross-legged or in Half Lotus position (see page 101), with your knees as close to the floor as you can, spine straight.
- Breathe in deeply through your nose and block your ears with one finger on each side.
- Close your mouth but keep your teeth apart.

- As you breathe out slowly and steadily through your mouth, make a long, strong, humming sound like a bee – mmmmmmmm.

- Listen to the sound inside you and feel the vibrations that the sound creates. This has a very soothing and calming effect.

- Try making other sounds like aaaah, oooo, eeee. Does it change where you feel the vibration? Try making loud then quiet noises.

The 'Ha' Breath

This breath gets rid of stale air in the lungs which results from shallow breathing.

- Lie down flat on your back, feet falling outwards comfortably, arms on the floor stretched above your head. Breathe in slowly and deeply.

- As you breathe out fast through your mouth, making the sound 'Ha!', bend your knees up onto your chest and bring your arms down to hug them against your chest.

- Breathe in again slowly as you stretch out flat again.

- Breathe normally for a moment before you do it again.

- Repeat three times.

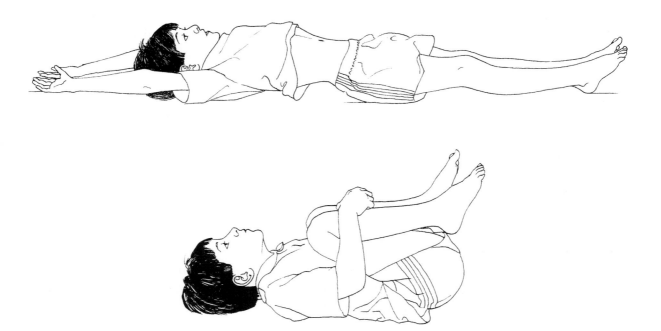

Hissing Balloon Breath

- Sit cross-legged in the Half Lotus position (see page 101), knees as close to the floor as you can, spine straight.
- Fold your tongue back onto the roof of your mouth, clench your teeth together and draw your lips apart as far as possible.
- Breathe in as deeply as you can, drawing the air through your teeth, as if you are filling your stomach like a balloon. 'Hiss!'. Close your lips and breathe out through your nose.
- Repeat three times.

This is really good to practise when you are hot and need to cool down. Notice how cold your tongue feels.

Alternate Nostril Breathing or Nadi shodana: only for children from eight upwards

This breathing practice has a balancing effect on the left and right sides of the brain. It therefore helps to bring the mind into the perfect state for learning – relaxed yet alert. With practice it becomes possible to control the air flow without using thumb and fingers.

- Sit comfortably in easy cross-legged position, rest your left hand, palm up or down on your knee.
- Breathe in first, then with your right hand close your left nostril with your third and fourth fingers and breathe out through your right nostril. If you are left-handed, use your other hand.
- Breathe in again through the right nostril. Release the left nostril. Now close your right nostril with your thumb and breathe out and then in again through your left nostril.

If a child has a cold and a blocked nose ask them to sit and get their hands in position but just to imagine the technique and the feel of doing the Alternate Nostril Breath. Soon it will become possible to give it a try.

Blowing Feathers and Ping Pong Balls

- Breathe in and with your outbreath through a straw, see if you can blow a feather along the floor, up in the air and towards someone waiting to catch it. Try the same with a ping pong ball, although you will only be able to hop it just off the ground. *Have fun!*

Staircase Breathing: only for children of eight upwards

- Look at this diagram with steps going up on one side and a smooth, quiet escalator coming down on the other.
- Imagine that you are going up and down these steps and up and down this escalator just by the way you breathe.

Now choose!

- If you are feeling tense or tired or short of energy, breathe yourself up the stairs by breathing in (with pauses, as you climb each step) and breathing out steadily as you come down again smoothly on the escalator. Use one full breath in as you imagine yourself climbing up the steps and one full breath out as you imagine yourself coming down the escalator.
- If you are feeling restless and it's hard to keep still for a moment, breathe in fully and deeply as you go up the escalator and breathe out as you come down the stairs, with a pause on each step.

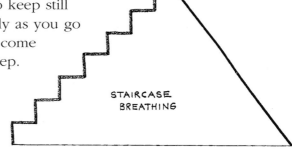

- Use one full breath in as you imagine yourself going up on the escalator and one full breath out as you come down the steps.

Practise both to begin with, then follow your choice for five breaths.

The Woodchopper or Kashtha Takshanasana

> *It cleans out and improves your lungs when you do breathing exercises. I like the Woodchopper pose.*
>
> Nine year old

- Sit in a squatting position with your feet as flat on the floor as you can. Your knees should be fully bent and separated.
- Clasp fingers of both hands together as if you are holding the handle of a woodchopper. Place your clasped hands on the floor between your feet. Straighten your arms and keep them straight throughout the practice.
- Now imagine the action of chopping wood. Raise your arms as high as possible above your head, stretching your spine upwards.
- Make a downward stroke with your arms as if chopping wood. Expel your breath as you do this, making a 'Ha' sound to empty all the air from your lungs. Hands back on the floor between your feet.
- Repeat three to five times.

Breathing and the Emotions

> *I felt my heart slowing down and I felt peace in the air and in me.*
>
> 12 year old

Different emotions also affect children's breathing patterns. Anger leads to faster breathing and faster breathing fuels the anger and keeps it going. Misery and sadness often result in shallow breathing and shallow breathing can hold the sadness in place. Whenever your child is showing a strong emotion, try to notice the way he is breathing, as this may give you the first clue towards giving the help he needs.

The following two techniques can be a first step in bringing calm to a stressed child.

The Magic Five Breaths Technique — to reduce stress, anxiety and fear

- Hold up your hand with fingers and thumb stretched wide as five candles and invite a younger child to take in a deep breath and blow out one candle with each new breath.

- Tip each finger down only when all the breath in the lungs has been blown out.

- Help older children to count backwards from five to one. Breathing right in and right out again is one count. It takes about five breaths to begin to feel a sense of calm.

- When the child is calmer, talk together about his or her feelings.

Volcano — to reduce anger and frustration (all ages)

- The child stands with feet wider than hip width so that his/her legs make a triangle with the floor. Ask the child to bring the palms together in front of the heart and close his or her eyes.

- Gently say *"Think of the feeling which is troubling you. Get yourself ready to explode your troubled feelings out and away like a volcano about to erupt. As you slowly raise your arms as high as possible above your head, keeping your palms together, take a slow, deep breath in through your nose. Then, burst out all your breath through your mouth with a loud noise and throw your arms out in a great wide circle. Imagine your hurtful feelings flying off in all directions.*

  Now stand quietly with your feet together and arms down, as still and strong as a mountain. Breathe slowly and gently. Listen to your body and mind become still and quiet. You may want to imagine something calm and beautiful like a place you love or a gentle animal."

- You may need to repeat this exercise over a few days if the anger or frustration resurfaces. Encourage your child to notice and identify any effects from the exercise.

CHAPTER 8

Relaxation

Children need to relax, and not just in front of the television! Their minds and bodies need a pause and a chance to centre.

Many medical and scientific studies on the effects of relaxation practice confirm the special benefits. Regular practice brings a new awareness and self-understanding, better concentration, physical and mental ease and a general sense of well-being. It helps children to listen and learn and to be aware of their emotions. Relaxation also gives children time to assimilate and absorb the day's activities. It distances them from their problems and can help them find a fresh perspective. This can be a great release from niggling anxieties.

Complete relaxation

How do we teach children to relax?

Some of the children are learning how to relax properly for the first time in their lives.

Primary teacher

A good way to begin is to explore relaxation and what it means through peaceful games.

Start a relaxation session by inviting the children to lie down, using the same form of words to help them settle down quickly.

For example:

"It's time to be still. It's time to be quiet. Lie down in Savasana [Relaxation Pose, see page 112]. Feel your whole body relax as you breathe out."

Using the same words each time becomes part of the process of deep relaxation.

Here are four ideas to start you off.

Sleeping Cats

Children lie like a sleeping cat on their sides with their knees tucked onto their chests, pretending to be asleep. To help them relax and to hold their attention, walk among them and tell a story describing a scene from nature. After a few sentences of the story you bring in the word 'mouse' and the children have to jump up as quickly as possible into The Cat pose (see page 96). This game teaches the children to remain alert yet relaxed; this is something which the cat family are experts at. This is a good game for children under the age of eight.

The Spaghetti Test

Children work in pairs. One child lies on the floor in the relaxation posture (see page 112), and relaxes as much as possible. The second child then checks how relaxed she is by gently lifting each arm and leg in turn. If the child is really relaxed she should feel like cooked spaghetti, limp and floppy. Each limb must be returned gently to the floor. If the limb is still tense, it will feel taut like uncooked spaghetti. Sometimes just having someone lifting the limbs helps the child to bring awareness to that body part and then she is able to relax it. The children then swap places.

Switch On/Switch Off

Each child has a switch on each foot, one 'off' and one 'on'. Talk the children through the settling stage of relaxation – *"Make sure you are comfortable, have a good stretch on the floor and then become still. I'm going to walk around and switch the 'off' button on your foot which means you are ready to relax and listen to a short story. At the end of the story I will walk around and press the 'on' button which means you can stretch and start to move slowly."* This works well with children up to the age of eight.

Butterfly Landing

Once the children are lying down comfortably ask them to imagine a beautiful blue butterfly. Then, calling out the name of a body part, tell them to imagine the butterfly landing on that body part and at the same time notice how that part of the body becomes relaxed. The visualization of the butterfly helps children to focus their attention on each part of their body in turn.

Begin and end each relaxation exercise with the same words so that there is a familiarity for the children which will give them reassurance and comfort.

Relaxation outside with grass and trees and water in all weathers and for as long as possible is perhaps the best way of all to get children and ourselves feeling relaxed and happy.

> *Yoga isn't just exercises for your body and your mind – it also stretches your spirit!*

Ten year old

Visualization

Visualization is an effective learning tool which increases concentration and memory skills and improves children's learning. The use of positive relaxing pictures helps to reduce stress.

When we are talking to children, we can tell them … *one way to help yourself become really relaxed is to look at peaceful pictures inside your head, while you lie in Savasana [Relaxation Pose]*.

You can help by describing one of your own favourite places to a child or group of children … perhaps by the sea, with warm sand and rippling waves and sea-birds calling – or beside the fire with delicious food on a plate – or beside a tumbling stream on a hillside with ferns and butterflies. Make it a place full of special colours, sounds, sights, smells, movement and a feeling of peace and happiness.

Alternatively, describe a series of little scenes or objects for children to see, in turn, in their imagination – with a six-second pause between each picture to give them enough time to enjoy it!

See a beautiful great tree on a hill with its leaves shimmering green and silver in the breeze [pause]. Now watch a brown bird fly away over a great valley [pause]. Now you are stroking a cat with white paws and listening to it purring and purring [pause]. Now you are walking on the grass in a park, the Sun is shining warm on your head, all the people are smiling at you and you can hear the ducks quacking to each other on the water [pause] and now you are watching a baby rabbit hopping through the grass [pause].

Peaceful Places

Sometimes invite the children just to lie completely still and go to a peaceful place in their imagination and see their own pictures. Gentle music played at the same time will help the children to relax and to visualize better. The children may wish to choose their own music. It doesn't matter whether they share where they have been and what they have seen afterwards or keep it to themselves. Tell them they can do just as they feel.

Worry Tree

This is a useful tool for children who find it hard to relax because of anxious worries or thoughts. Invite them to think about whether there is anything worrying them and then to imagine putting their anxieties and worries into a little basket and hanging it on a tree. "*The tree will look after your worries while you relax in peace!*" This idea is described in Maureen Garth's book *Sunshine* (see page 167).

A flower for meditation

CHAPTER 9

Meditation and mandalas

Yoga practice can help you to discover your own inner peace and inner strength through meditation. This becomes your own best preparation for every day of your life.

Meditation gives children a time of stillness and peace

Statues and paintings of ancient rishis often show them sitting cross-legged with the tips of their fingers touching the tips of their thumbs to form a circle. A rishi or yogi, when meditating or resting, may join the tips of his thumbs with the tips of his first fingers to make an electrical circuit, so that energy is not seeping away but is kept flowing to recharge the body. The Indian word for such special ways of moving or holding the hands is a 'mudra'.

When you are meditating using the Half Lotus or Full Lotus, close your eyes and turn hands palms upwards with tips of thumbs and first fingers touching. Bring knees a little closer together.

Here is one meditation exercise for you to try.

Candle-flame Relaxation and Meditation

WARNING: A child suffering from epilepsy should not focus on a flickering flame. Make sure children are at a safe distance from the candle.

If you would like a change from the usual yoga relaxation exercises or want to celebrate a special occasion (someone's birthday, festival time, the end of term or completion of a series of yoga classes) here is a very special way to end.

Have ready a candle for each child, gentle background music and a specially chosen poem or short reading. A birthday cake candle will do, stuck upright in a saucer with some sticky tack; or a child could focus instead on a beautiful, still object of the child's choice, such as a flower or pebble or picture.

Invite the children to sit with you in a circle, in the Lotus position if comfortable, with the curtains drawn and the lights dimmed, a lit candle on the floor in front of each child.

Ask the children to look at their candle flame for a few moments then to close their eyes and concentrate on the 'after image', trying to see it as clearly as they can. When this fades, suggest they open their eyes and look at the real flame again to make the 'after image' stronger once more. This exercise counterbalances the quick glance habit that children develop through watching television with its hectic speed of light and scene change and visual shock tactics.

When a feeling of peaceful concentration has filled the room and there's no sound but the music, start reading the poem or piece you have chosen.

When you have finished reading, leave the music playing into the silence for another minute or two, then gently rouse the children by telling them that you are going to let the daylight back into the room (or put the lights back on) and that it's time to open their eyes and to blow out their candles.

This exercise beautifully demonstrates the unity of mind, body and spirit. The children experience being still on both the inside and the outside, and being alone with their little light, yet in company.

With older children you can explain that the candle flame represents their inner spirit which will grow stronger through practising yoga, just as they can learn to hold the image of the flame more and more brightly in their mind with their eyes closed.

After this exercise children usually go back to the ordinary day refreshed by a feeling of thoughtfulness and peace.

Candle meditation

> *Peace can work miracles. It makes you a happy and lovely person. Peace goes out from you to other people.*

Marguerite Smithwhite

MANDALAS

I colour mandalas before I go to sleep when my head is too full.

Lizzie, aged 13

Absorbed in colouring a mandala

A mandala (which means both circle and centre) is a symbolic circular design that represents both the world outside ourselves that we can see (the circle) and the invisible world (the centre) which lies hidden in our hearts and minds. Mandalas are often used as a focus for meditation.

Mandalas have been found on the walls of prehistoric caves, in ancient tapestries and stained glass windows and in the drawings and paintings of people all over the world. They can be very simple or incredibly complex in their design. In their simplest form, they are used to decorate the home or clothing. Tibetan monks make incredibly intricate and delicate mandalas for their important ceremonies, sometimes out of coloured sand and rice instead of paper and paint.

Mandalas contain themes and patterns taken from anything in the natural environment such as rings on a cut tree trunk and the shapes from shells and flowers. Ideas are also taken from geometry and folk art.

The process of colouring a mandala is calming and focusing. As soon as children become deft with a crayon or paintbrush and are able to colour in shapes with enough precision to be satisfying, they will usually become deeply absorbed.

For older children and adults, the designing, the drawing and the colouring of a mandala serve to help in the search for fulfilment and happiness because it gives us, at our fingertips, a way to begin connecting with everything in our lives. This awakens us to new possibilities inside ourselves and outside ourselves. Our own careful mandala can have a magnetic quality which warms us every time we look at it.

- Start at the centre, or the outer edge, with the bright colours – all the different reds, oranges and yellows. These colours stimulate our minds and give us energy to concentrate.
- Move on, through all the different colours and shades, till you are finally using calming blues and greens and softer tones like peach to complete the centre or the outer rim of your mandala, whichever way you have chosen to work.
- A ruler and compass or different sized mugs and bowls to draw circles will be needed when children decide to design their own mandalas.

As children work through shifts in colour and tone and build the beautiful patterns, they begin to discover the stored wisdom and knowledge which every person holds in the deeper, subconscious parts of their minds. This wisdom and intuitive understanding about life and healing is stored in us in the shape of symbols – and these same symbols will surface and become visible when we create a mandala for ourselves.

Looking closely at a mandala and colouring it in, whether it is your own creation entirely or a given pattern, becomes a time of peaceful meditation.

Make sure there is time for children to study their completed mandalas carefully and unhurriedly and then put them up somewhere where they can see them every day for a while.

Photocopy the mandalas on pages 158–160 to get you started.

A 'garden' of yoga poses

Yoga practice is a sensitive and powerful tool for living. All we are doing when we are teaching yoga to children is working for a state of balance. This balance of body, mind and emotions is what will bring about each child's delight and respect for his or her own body. It is this feeling that helps children learn respect and care for other people. They have a right, and a need to learn this life-long self-respect. It will allow their spirit to shine.

Yoga Means Wholeness

To do yoga
means to try very
hard to make every part
of you as perfect as possible.
Ready for anything that might happen.
It means to help your physical body to
be graceful and strong in form and movement;
to give it only sensible food; not to destroy
any part of it with alcohol, smoking or drugs;
to keep it clean, as well as the places where it lives,
works and plays. It means to develop your life energy
by creative activities; to listen to beautiful music;
to look at beautiful things; to draw and paint and
dance and to make things of value and beauty.
It means not giving in to every want, but
considering whether what you want to do
is good both for yourself and for
other people; to try always to
be kind and never cruel; to
be honest in small as well
as big ways. It means
to try to control your
thoughts to bring
stillness and
peace into
your mind
and heart.
It means to
remember
that your
life has
a special
purpose.
In this
way
everything
you do
will be
your
yoga.

You could colour this and put it up on your bedroom wall or write it up in large letters and turn it into it into a long-tailed kite that you can fly!

Appendix 1

A fuller exploration of Patanjali's Eightfold Path

Yamas and niyamas are the building blocks towards achieving the benefits of yoga for everyone, young and old.

YAMAS

There are five yamas. They are about social disciplines – the ways we behave towards other people.

- **Ahimsa means non-violence**

  Being kind; taking turns; not hurting anyone or anything; trying not to be mean by unkind teasing, name-calling or bullying. Be open and willing to listen and talk to others for understanding rather than conflict. Peace begins with yourself, inside your head.

  Parents can help by preventing their children from watching violent television programmes and videos, playing violent video games and using toy killer weapons in their play. Modelling non-violent behaviour and out-spoken apology and forgiveness is the best teaching of all. Children need to be helped and shown how to cope with anger and conflict by talking openly about them and learning strategies to help them turn away from aggressive behaviour.

- **Satya means truthfulness**

  No lies or fibs. Not hurting another's feelings with untrue and unkind tales. Satya is about deciding to tell the truth rather than lying or being deceitful. People who tell the truth are trusted and admired. It's often hard to tell the truth because of fear, but it's easier to love those who have the courage to do so.

Parents can help their children to be truthful by modelling truthfulness in their own behaviour and encouraging children to be open. It helps children a great deal if adults always let them know how much they value and respect them for their truthfulness.

- **Asteya means no-stealing, being honest**

  Not taking anything that is not yours without permission. There are the more obvious kinds of stealing such as shoplifting and more subtle kinds such as stealing the ideas of someone else, for example copying someone else's work at school or taking credit for something that should go to someone else.

  Parents can help by being honest themselves, even in the smallest ways and by helping children to be aware of the more subtle ways of stealing that surround us all and may be ignored.

- **Brahmacharya means moderation and self-control**

  Honouring parents by following family rules and helping willingly with household jobs; being willing to let other people be the focus of attention.

  Parents can help by keeping things in perspective and not giving in to a child's pestering to buy more clothes, toys and treats than is sensible and deserved. This also means parents modelling simplicity at home and in their own behaviour. It helps to discuss with the children the poverty and needs of children in other places and encouraging their own children to be thoughtful and generous.

- **Aparigraha means no greed or grasping, being generous**

  Not 'needing' lots of possessions – such as toys and clothes – to be happy; taking care of the things you do have and being willing to give away what you have outgrown.

  Aparigraha also means not eating more than the body needs.

  Parents can help by discovering with their children the origins of different foods and the importance of fresh, whole produce. Children can be helped throughout their childhood to develop healthy and regular eating habits and to recognize when they have had enough. Preparing food and cooking meals together can be fun and is an important life skill which will benefit them when they grow up and leave home.

NIYAMAS

There are five niyamas. These are personal disciplines set down by Patanjali about the way we care for ourselves and how we develop self-control.

- **Saucha means purity**

  Saucha is the practice of cleanliness which encourages self-respect. Parents can teach children to keep their bodies, hair, teeth and nails clean. They should also encourage children to keep their rooms clean and to help with other chores so that their home is fresh and welcoming to others.

  Playing outside in the sunshine and fresh air, and getting enough exercise and sleep – and eating fresh, healthy food that isn't processed or loaded with chemicals – is part of that purity. Cultivating kind thoughts and doing thoughtful acts for others without being asked is also saucha.

- **Santosha means contentment**

  Children can learn to accept even when things don't go their way or when sad things happen to them. Santosha means not holding back but being generous and unselfish. It means being grateful for what you have. Children can, if encouraged, find happiness in each day, even when things don't turn out as planned. One of the best ways to cultivate contentment is to recognize and respect your own needs and work out how you can give yourself enough time each day – even short pauses – to relax and re-energize. Do what you enjoy doing for a while and tell your children why you are enjoying doing this. With this sense of contentment, everyone in the family can feel happier and more fulfilled.

- **Tapas means self-discipline**

  Tapas is about trying our best; taking responsibility for what we do and think and say. It means trying to do and be our best at home, at school and wherever else we may be. Self-discipline is a skill that improves with practice.

  Children have a strong instinct to please their parents, their teachers and their friends. This is the start of self-discipline. Children also learn self-discipline through playing in organized sport, practising for music lessons, having certain treats only on certain days, and by helping care for younger children, pets and plants. They learn by doing what their parents and teachers tell them until they are old enough to do things, such as chores and homework, without being constantly reminded.

- **Svadhyaya means self-observation and self-study**

  This niyama is about self-study – thinking about the things you are doing and your thoughts and feelings. This means talking and writing about them so you know better who you are and how you are growing and changing. It means sharing your feelings with your parents and friends, trying to overcome negative emotions like being sulky and cross and finding better ways to manage difficulties. It means working things out for yourself rather than giving in to pressure from your friends.

  Parents can help by making sure there are peaceful opportunities every day for each child to be able to talk with them and to know they are heard and valued.

- **Ishwarapranidhana means finding a sense of divinity**

  This niyama is about becoming aware that there is a source of love and good in the world and that, through conscious living, we can deepen our connection with that source. We come to recognize this through noticing that we are happiest when we are serving and doing good things for others.

PRATYAHARA

This is calming and stilling the senses for a deep peace.

Children learn everything through their senses; however, too much information can be exhausting and problematic. Being able to focus on the senses enables children to develop an inner stillness and outer calm which then enhances concentration.

DHARANA

This is increasing concentration by focusing full attention.

Many children are over-stimulated or stressed by problems at home and become unable to concentrate for more than a moment or two. The speed of television and computer images also sabotages children's ability to concentrate. However, children can be taught to focus on one thing only, such as their favourite flower, fruit, pet, bird, picture, shell, colour or shape. As well as increasing a child's ability to concentrate, this will also balance out negative feelings or thoughts by bringing moments of calm and stillness into their day.

DHYANA

This is the practice of meditation.

After calming the senses and learning how to concentrate better, meditation follows naturally. Those meditating begin to feel still and at one with whatever is the focus of their meditation, for example a candle flame or a beautiful stone.

SAMADHI

Samadhi is finding the joy and bliss which is there in our hearts.

This is the final achievement on the Eightfold Path which usually can only happen for us when the rest of the Eightfold Path has been travelled, step by step.

When our values and actions are founded in love, when control over the body, the breath, the senses and the mind has been practised and mastered, the result will be a deep sense of contentment. This sense of connectedness, of belonging, of happiness will be there for every child and adult who practises yoga, and every family who walks the yoga path.

ASANAS and PRANAYAMA, the other two stages of the Eightfold Path, are covered in chapters 6 and 7.

Appendix 2

Qualified teachers and training opportunities

Qualified yoga teachers

Fully qualified yoga teachers are professionally trained in applied anatomy and physiology and understand structural kinesiology so that they can modify the postures to suit the different abilities of the children. Through the training they also learn how to plan lessons, starting from warm-ups at the beginning, how to build up a yoga programme for the children and the step-by-step care required for the closing down stages.

If you are interested in inviting a children's yoga teacher into your school, or if you are interested in training as a children's yoga teacher yourself, contact The British Wheel of Yoga, RYE, YOU & ME Yoga for Children with Special Needs or YogaBuds.

Training opportunities

There are now four well-known training courses for anyone who wishes to teach yoga to children. It is hoped that all reputable and long-established schools of yoga will also now extend their yoga courses to include children's yoga teacher training.

The British Wheel of Yoga

The British Wheel of Yoga Training Module gives already qualified yoga teachers the additional and necessary skills, experience and confidence to set up and run yoga classes for children in a variety of settings. They will be ready and able to teach yoga to children and to introduce the concept of yoga in the classroom to heads, teachers and school governors as well as to parent groups.

The course comprises six whole day seminars, home study of about 35 hours in total and the experience of planning, setting up and running a yoga class for children.

The course covers:

- The physiological and psychological aspects of teaching yoga to children.
- Practical sessions of asanas and pranayamas.
- Relaxation techniques and other practices which improve attention, concentration and memory.
- Group-work and plenary sessions.
- Group discussions concerned with children's age, their range of ability, their special needs.
- RYE (Research on Yoga in Education) and support available to help teachers begin yoga practices with their children.

Five written assignments must be submitted for assessment and a British Wheel of Yoga certificate will be presented on successful completion of the course.

British Wheel of Yoga Central Office
25 Jermyn Street
Sleaford
Lincs NG34 7RU
Tel: 01529 306851

www.bwy.org.uk
email: office@bwy.org.uk

The British Wheel of Yoga is the governing body for yoga in Great Britain and is recognized by Sport England. It acts as an umbrella organization for other yoga groups. The following schools of yoga are already accredited or affiliated to the British Wheel of Yoga.

The Association of Yoga Studies (AYS)
The Satyananda Yoga School (SYS)
The Mandala Yoga Ashram (MYA)
Inner Yoga Trust
Yoga Scotland
Sunpower Yoga
The Life Centre

Contact details for these are available through the British Wheel of Yoga.

Research on Yoga in Education (RYE)

RYE was established in Paris by Micheline Flak in the 1970s. It was created to give teachers expert training in yoga techniques. By the 1990s it was being translated into different languages and spreading from continent to continent. The success of her work with children is now reflected in the experience of teachers in many countries who have followed her techniques. RYE training programmes now exist around the world to teach the RYE techniques to teachers, to network between different countries and to gather feedback.

The RYE diploma is a two-year course comprising nine weekends and one week residential:

Year One: Techniques of yoga in school
Year Two: Techniques of relaxation

The course is open to teachers from different educational levels (nursery, primary, secondary, university), teaching assistants, special needs teachers, parents, doctors, paediatricians, nurses, educational psychologists, speech therapists, teachers of yoga and associated disciplines such as tai chi and chi kung (meditation, body alignment and breathing techniques). Trainees must attend a weekly yoga class during the course.

Through RYE training, yoga can be informally introduced by the children's class teacher just through using a few basic yoga and relaxation techniques infused into the lessons. This will steady and calm the children and get them into a receptive state of mind and ready to learn.

RYE diploma holders can do INSETs in school for teachers and use RYE techniques in the classroom or at home. The RYE diploma only qualifies you to teach RYE techniques; you will not be qualified to teach full yoga classes to children until you have also trained through the British Wheel of Yoga, YOU & ME Yoga or YogaBuds.

> The RYE diploma is internationally valid in all the RYE centres (UK, France, Belgium, Italy, Germany, Greece, Uruguay, Israel).
> www.ryeuk.org
> Contact email: lynnparrott@rye.uk.org

YOU & ME Yoga for Children with Special Needs

YOU & ME Yoga Training for parents, carers and teachers is given in their homes, schools, specialist units, community centres and clubs by a trained YOU & ME Trainer.

Level 1   Introductory YOU & ME Yoga Trainers training

Level 2   Assessment. Joint Looseness and Relaxation for Special Needs

Level 3   YOU & ME Yoga Postures and Breathing for Special Needs

The advantages of YOU & ME Yoga training are that it is inexpensive to run; the adults and children all learn and share yoga together and it is of personal benefit to everyone. It improves children's quality of life by increasing their mobility, dexterity, co-ordination, concentration, adaptive behaviour, communication, sensory awareness and self-confidence.

These introductory books with a DVD / video can be seen and bought online:

Introduction to YOU & ME Yoga.
Learning Difficulties and Associated Conditions Explained, with Yoga Case Studies.
The Origin of the YOU & ME Yoga System.
Distance Learning programme.

Details about the books, the training and the course materials can be reviewed on the website.

Contact
Maria Gunstone
YOU & ME Yoga
PO Box 39259
London SE3 0XJ
www.youandmeyoga.com

YogaBuds

YogaBuds offers an Edexcel accredited BTEC Advanced Diploma for Teaching Yoga to Children.

YogaBuds provides yoga teaching in mainstream primary and special needs schools throughout the UK. In these schools, yoga teaching becomes an integral part of the school day. It has had a remarkable effect on thousands of children with ADHD and autism. The children show marked improvements in communication skills, greater calm in difficult situations and develop their ability to relax.

The training course places particular emphasis on working empathetically and creatively with children. It links yoga to many areas of the National Curriculum.

YogaBuds Ltd
47 Algers Road
Loughton
Essex IG10 4NG
Tel: 020 8508 3653
www.yogabuds.org.uk
info@yogabuds.org.uk

Child protection

Check that any training course you do covers child development and has a Child Protection Policy in place. Everyone teaching yoga to other people's children in the UK will need an Enhanced Disclosure (police confirmation) and insurance to cover their practice.

For the development of your own yoga practice

Contact the British Wheel of Yoga or one of its accredited yoga groups or the Iyengar Institute.

The Iyengar method of yoga practice was developed by Yogacharya Sri B. K. S. Iyengar near Puna in India. The many years' training commitment and the rigorous assessment process which goes into becoming a certified Iyengar yoga teacher is one of the reasons for Iyengar Yoga becoming the world's most widely practised method of yoga. As well as the 900 Iyengar yoga teachers in the UK and Ireland, there are many Iyengar yoga associations worldwide.

The Iyengar method focuses on precision, alignment and safety in each posture. It builds strength, flexibility, stamina and balance. It would be particularly suitable for children who like to keep fit and it is hoped that a specific training course for working with children will soon be in place. By 2006 Iyengar had already been introduced into several schools across the UK.

Iyenga Yoga Institute, Maida Vale
223a Randolph Avenue
London W9 1NL
Tel: 020 7624 3080
www.iyi.org.uk
office@iyi.org.uk

This

Merit Certificate

was presented to

....

for

Basic Yoga

Signed

Date

Mandala

A decorative scroll of birds and beasts for children to colour

Glossary

Ahimsa	Non-violence
Aparigraha	Generosity, learning to live with only a few possessions
Asanas	Physical postures/exercises
Asteya	Non-stealing
Brahmacharya	Self-control
Dharana	Concentration
Dhyana	Meditation (contemplation)
Hatha yoga	The way of physical training to prepare the mind and body for meditation
Ishwarapranidhana	A sense of divinity
Mandala	'Whole world' or 'healing circle'; it is a symbol for connection, meditation, protection and healing. It is often drawn like a palace with four gates facing the four corners of the world
Mudra	The Indian word for a special way of holding or moving the hands
Niyama	The five personal disciplines of cleanliness, contentment, great effort, self-knowledge, faith in a higher power
Pranayama	Controlled breath
Pratyahara	Control of the senses (taste, touch and hearing)
Rishi	A great sage or wise man in tune with himself and nature
Samadhi	Enlightenment (a sense of absolute unity with all creation)
Sankalpa	Positive affirmation
Sanskrit	Sanskrit is one of the oldest languages in the world. All India's ancient and holy writings are in Sanskrit
Santosha	Contentment, satisfaction
Satya	Truthfulness
Saucha	Purity, cleanliness
Svadhyaya	Self-knowledge
Tapas	Being humble and penitent for wrong-doing
Yama	The five social disciplines of non-violence, truth, honesty, self-control, generosity
Yoga	Union or yoke
Yogi	A male practitioner of yoga
Yogini	A female practitioner of yoga

Resources

Useful Books

Helping Children with Yoga is one of the series of *Right from the Start* guides for parents and teachers. If this book has been helpful and fun you might enjoy other books in the series which are planned to follow this one:

Stillness, Imagination and Meditation for Children by Sarah Woodhouse with Marguerite Smithwhite and Clare Finka This book is about helping children develop their inner life and to realize their power to love, to give comfort and to create beauty. It is also about healing through meditation and art. It is full of helpful and interesting ideas.

Touch, Massage and Movement, Deepening the connection with children. Based on the work being done by Carla Hannaford in the USA and schools in the UK and Sweden where peer massage is a normal daily practice.

For more information on the publication of other books in the *Right from the Start* series, see
www.rightfromthestart.co.uk
www.networkcontinuum.co.uk (Network Continuum Education)
www.hawthornpress.com (Hawthorn Press)

Berry, J. (2001), *Around the World in 80 Poems*, illustrated by Catherine Lucas, Macmillan Children's Books, London

Bersma, D. and Visscher, M. (2003), *Yoga Games for Children*, Hunter House Publishers, Alameda, Canada
A useful book with 68 ideas, games and examples to use as variations when teaching yoga to children. From 3 years old to 12 years old. The book covers co-operation and trust games as well as games for yoga postures, breathing, relaxation and meditation.

Browne, P.A. (1995), *African Animals ABC*, Barefoot Books, Bath
Some useful rhymes to enjoy with the animal postures.

Burman, E. (1997), *Whose Eyes are These?*, STL Publishers, USA

Burningham, J. (2001), *Mr Gumpy's Outing*, Red Fox Picture Books, London

Burrell, A. and Riley, J. (eds) (2005), *The Right from the Start Handbook for Teachers: Promoting Children's Well-Being in the Primary Years*, Network Educational Press, Stafford
A book filled with all sorts of innovative approaches, able to give children a flying start. There are dozens of imaginative, tried-and-tested ideas, strategies and activities with real 'soul' which might be missing from the school curriculum.

Chanchani, S. and Chanchani, R. (1995), *Yoga for Children*, UBS Publishers Distributors Limited, Delhi, India
A thorough and comprehensive Indian guide to yoga. The authors trace the roots of yoga through Indian legends and mythology. This book presents a very comprehensive range of postures.

Cohen, K. and Hyme, J. (1992), *Imagine That: Child's Guide to Yoga*, Integral Yoga Publications, USA
A book for parents to use with their children. The magical poems and illustrations in this book of yoga postures will capture the imagination as well as introduce children to hatha yoga. For ages 4-14.

Curtis, C. (2005), *I Took the Moon for a Walk*, Barefoot Books, Bath

Curtiss, A.B. (1994), *In the Company of Bears*, Old Castle Publishing, California, USA

Donaldson, J. (2005), *Wriggle and Roar!*, Macmillan Children's Books, London
Rhymes for yoga stories.

Gerstein, M. (1987), *The Mountains of Tibet, A child's journey through living and dying*, Barefoot Books, Bath
A warm, imaginative and comforting story.

Gugler, L.D. (2003), *There's a Billy Goat in the Garden*, Barefoot Books, Bath

Harter, D. (illustrator) **and Penner, F.** (2005), *The Animal Boogie* Barefoot Books, Bath
CD with book.

Hill, L.D. (2001), *Connecting Kids: Exploring Diversity Together*, New Society Publishers, British Columbia, Canada
A practical and fun resource for resolving and celebrating our differences. An excellent and imaginative guidebook full of co-operative games, creative activities and nature experiences.

Hund, W. (2001), *42 Mandala patterns*, Hunter House, Alameda, Calif.
For teachers, parents and children. Mandalas to colour for inspiration and to create a calm atmosphere.

Khalsa, S.K. (1998), *Fly Like a Butterfly: Yoga for children*, Sterling Juvenile Books, New York
An ideal book for a child (from three years old).

Komitor, J.B. (2000), *The Complete Idiot's Guide to Yoga with Kids*, Alpha Books, Indianapolis, USA
A practical and comprehensive book on children's yoga including lots of fun and games. There is a chapter about each age group and practical advice for parents.

Lark, L. (2003), *Yoga for Kids*, Carlton Books, London
All stages of yoga are explored and explained in this book. The author introduces each posture with a story.

Lupton, H. (2003), *The Gingerbread Man*, Barefoot Books, Bath
Beautifully developed and illustrated, age-old rhythmic tale of the hungry animals.

Mainland, P. (1998), *Yoga Parade of Animals*, Element Books Inc, Boston, USA
A colourful book for young children just beginning yoga. Clear and easy to read.

Mayo, D. (illustrator) (2001), *The House that Jack Built*, Barefoot Books, Bath
Some useful rhymes to enjoy with the animal postures.

Mitton, J. and Balit, C. (1998), *Zoo in the Sky*, Francis Lincoln, London
A book of animal constellations.

Rice, D.L. (2000), *Do Animals Have Feelings Too?*, Dawn Publications, Nevada City, California

Simpson, L.J. (2001), *Into the Garden of Dreams: Pathways to imagination for 5–8s*, Brilliant Publications, Dunstable, Bedfordshire

Singleton, M. (2004), *Yoga for You and Your Child*, Duncan Baird Publishers, London
A book which makes yoga sessions child friendly with games, 'yoga adventures' and imitating animal walks and noises as well as shapes. Covers topics such as stress and illness.

Smith, A. (1998), *Accelerated Learning in Practice: Brain-based methods for accelerating motivation and achievement*, Network Educational Press, Stafford

Smith, A. (2002), *Move It: Physical Movement and Learning*, Network Educational Press Stafford
Exercises to stretch the mind and brain.

Stewart, M. and Phillips, K. (1992), *Yoga for Children*, Vermilion, London
This book has exceptionally clear and helpful photographs of children working with adults and descriptions of each posture.

Sumar, S. (1998), *Yoga for the Special Child*, Special Yoga Publications, Buckingham, Virginia, USA
This book offers an easy to follow therapeutic programme for parents, educators, yoga teachers and healthcare professionals to use with children with learning and developmental disabilities. There is a step-by-step, integrated system of yoga poses designed to increase cognitive and motor skills and breathing exercises to improve concentration.

Waddell, M. (1996), *The Big Big Sea*, Walker Books, London

Watts, L.J. (2002), *Spiritual Circles for harmony and fulfilment*, Hermes House, London

Meditation/Visualization Books

Fontana, D. and Slack, I. (1997), *Teaching Meditation to Children*, Element, Dorset
Aimed at parents, teachers and other adults who work with young people. It is an instructive read with information and practical exercises which children of all ages can appreciate and learn from. Includes meditations for psychological and social problems such as anxiety, aggression and hyperactivity.

Garth, M. (1991–1997), *Sunshine; Starbright; Moonbeam; The Inner Garden,*
HarperCollins, Melbourne, Australia
A series of gentle books containing imaginative visualizations to read with young children. They are useful to calm them, develop their imagination and help them learn how to relax.

Lindbergh, R. (2000), *In Every Tiny Grain of Sand*, Walker Books, London
A treasure-trove of poems and prayers from around the world which can bring a special touch to any yoga session. Can be used in PSHE or Literacy Hour.

Murdock, M. (1987), *Spinning Inward*, Shambala, Boston, USA
A book for parents and teachers who are interested in the use of guided imagery as an effective method of 'whole brain' learning. The techniques offered in this book are designed to help children tap into the wealth of their own innate creativity and wisdom.

Useful Props

Buckley, A. (2003), *The Kids' Yoga Deck*, Chronicle Books, San Francisco, USA
A very useful and versatile teaching tool. The deck consists of 50 cards, some of which are group and partner poses, sitting postures with a breathing technique and single postures.

Yoga mats are now available from many department stores and supermarkets, the internet and the British Wheel of Yoga.

Videos and DVDs

Irvine, E. (2003), *Yoga for Healthy Mother and Child*, Green Umbrella Productions
A down-to-earth holistic approach to yoga with the older child. Includes a discussion on eating well.

Wenig, M. (2004), *YogaKids3: Silly to Calm for ages 3–6,* Living Arts

Wenig, M. (2004), *YogaKids2: ABCs for ages 3–6,* Living Arts

Yoga for Children (2003), Quantum Leap Group Ltd, Cambridgeshire

Catalogue

Incentive Plus Ltd
6 Fernfield Farm
Little Harwood
Milton Keynes MK17 0PR
Tel: 01908 526120
www.incentiveplus.co.uk

Brings together in one catalogue all kinds of games and books for developing children's social, emotional and behaviourial skills and safeguarding their mental health. Incentive Plus is a curriculum online retailer linked to www.curriculumonline.gov.org

Recommended books and CDs available from Incentive Plus:

Hands On: How to use Brain Gym® in the classroom
by Isabel Cohen and Marcelle Goldsmith

Brain Gym® CD
Six different musical presentations for brain/body warm-up exercises. *Brain Gym® – Simple Activities* is the accompanying book.

Mozart for Accelerated Learning, CD Roland Roberts

Useful Organizations

British Wheel of Yoga
Central Office
25 Jermyn Street
Sleaford, Lincs NG34 7RU
Tel: 01529 306851   email: office@bwy.org.uk   www.bwy.org.uk

Research on Yoga in Education (RYE)
www.ryeuk.org
Contact email: lynnparrott@rye.uk.org

The National Asthma Campaign (NAC)
www.asthma-uk.co.uk   email: asthmauk@aol.com

Birthlight
PO Box 148
Cambridge CB4 2GB
Tel: 01223 362288   email: enquiries@birthlight.com   www.birthlight.com

The Birthlight Trust exists for the greater enjoyment of pregnancy, birth and babies. It runs ante-natal and post-natal yoga courses for mothers and also baby massage, baby yoga and infant aquatic classes for mothers and their babies.

Brain Gym®
Brain Gym® was researched and developed by Paul Dennison, a pioneer in applied brain research and an educator experienced in curriculum development and experimental psychology. It is a series of simple and sometimes unusual movements for children and adults, which enhance whole brain learning. They can be particularly helpful for children with learning difficulties and emotional problems (www.braingym.org.uk). Brain Gym® movements can also be used as an excellent warm-up exercise before yoga practice.

Accelerated Learning
Alistair Smith developed this child-friendly, fun approach to lessons (www.alite.co.uk). The four-stage Accelerated Learning Cycle which he devised for teachers also provides a useful framework for teachers who are developing their lesson plans for teaching yoga to children.

Websites

www.yogauk.com

www.kidsmusic.co.uk

www.youandme.yoga.com for children with special educational needs

www.circle-time.co.uk

Index

Also available from Network Continuum Education

Parenting

We are proud to introduce some key titles that provide aspiring parents with all they need to know in giving their children the best possible start in life, while preparing them for formal education.

Help Your Young Child to Succeed
The essential guide for parents of 3–5 year olds
Ros Bayley, Lynn Broadbent & Debbie Pullinger

'A marvellous book – informative, accessible and wise. Exactly what busy parents need to ensure the best possible start for their children.'
Sue Palmer, Education consultant and author

Following the success of Help Your Child to Succeed, this new title in the series focuses on how parents of 3-5-year-old children can help them enjoy learning as they head towards formal education. It presents the latest educational thinking about young children in a highly accessible and entertaining style, with quizzes, practical suggestions, tips and illustrated examples.

PB 1 85539 214 3, ISBN-13 978-18553-9214-4, 96pp, October 2006

Help Your Child to Succeed
Bill Lucas & Alistair Smith

'A valuable starting point that won't overwhelm your child.'
Junior Magazine, 2006

The book that has inspired parents to get involved in helping their children to enjoy learning. An essential guide for parents of foundation and primary age children with useful tips on what parents can do to motivate their child, how to manage their child's anger, helping their child to do well at the things they find difficult, how to best to communicate with their child and how to help with homework.

PB 1 85539 111 2, ISBN-13 978-18553-9111-6, 96pp, 2002

Flying Start with Literacy
Ros Bayley & Lyn Broadbent

'offer[s] useful starting ideas if you want to contribute to your child's learning.'
Junior Magazine, 2006

Good literacy skills are vital for success at school - but often the most important foundations are laid outside the classroom. This book tells parents and carers of three-to-seven year olds all they need to know about how to give children the best possible start in literacy. Packed with exciting games and activities, it shows why parental support makes such a difference, how to help a child become a good communicator, ways to encourage listening skills, how to develop literacy through music and movement, the benefits of reading to children and telling stories, what 'phonics' is all about and how to help children acquire the range of skills involved in learning to write.

PB 1 85539 194 5, ISBN-13 978-18553-9194-9, 96pp, 2005

Parents' and Carers' Guide for Able and Talented Children

Barry Teare

This book brings parents and carers right up to date with recent developments on the thinking about and provision for able and talented children. With expert guidance from Barry Teare, it advises how to provide more able children with the best possible opportunities, in partnership with schools and specialist organizations.

PB 1 85539 128 7, ISBN-13 978-18553-9128-4, 112pp, 2004

Getting your Little Darlings to Behave

'I wish Sue Cowley had been my teacher'
Families Online

'In this book I offer practical and realistic advice for parents about how to manage their children's behaviour. As with my books for teachers, it is written in a realistic and down to earth way. I give tips and strategies that will help you deal with all the behaviour issues that you face, from getting the basics right, through to dealing with more serious problems. As a teacher I've dealt with the behaviour of literally thousands of different children; as a parent I understand just how stressful managing behaviour 24/7 can be. The strategies that I outline in this book are simple to understand and put into practice, but will make an amazing difference to your children's behaviour.' Sue Cowley

PB 0 8264 9159 6, ISBN-13 978-08264-9159-6, 192pp, 2006

A Parent's Guide to Primary School

'Very easy to read and a great introduction into what you can expect your child to be studying and learning.'
My Child Magazine, August 2006

A well-written, compelling, meticulously researched resource for parents everywhere. A wonderfully comprehensive guide for parents, providing advice on every aspect of their child's education; from choosing a suitable school, to communicating with teachers, through to dealing with the trauma of homework.

PB 0 8264 7379 2, ISBN-13 978-08264-7379-0, 176pp, 2004